Advance praise for *Signed, Anonymous*

"Here is a long awaited book about a neglected topic that's actually one of Jesus' most liberating secrets for living life to the fullest: how to play our lives to an audience of One. This is an impelling book that will set you free of your need for recognition to enjoy the sheer delight of anonymity . . and the Lord's affirmation."

—LLOYD OGILVIE, former chaplain of the U.S. Senate,
best-selling author, pastor, Hollywood Presbyterian Church

"God is most impressed by folks who do good for Him alone, rather than showboats who play to the crowd. This book drives home this truth in unmistakable terms."

—SPARKY ANDERSON, Hall of Fame former manager,
Cincinnati Reds and Detroit Tigers

"We live in a culture where the arrows are all turned inward; what's in this for me? What will people think? How can I grab the spotlight or make sure I get the credit? The Kingdom of God, however, reverses this focus; the arrows are turned outward. Others become the focus. We are called to be of service rather than "successful." This is a wonderful book filled with fresh insight about a neglected topic: the power and joy of anonymous living. I was challenged and inspired!"

—JOHN C. BOWLING, president, Olivet Nazarene University

"Jon Johnston has written a great and much-needed book. Andy Warhol's "15-minutes of fame" can't begin to compete with the Christian joy of anonymous giving. You'll receive profound joy and inspiration from reading this book."

—WILLIAM S. BANOWSKY, former president, Pepperdine University
and the University of Oklahoma

"Bringing the realism of a scientist, an educator, and a Spirit-filled believer, Johnston knows that God's intention can often be short-circuited by the abrasions of popular culture. He explores anonymity as the road less traveled that can lead to delightful experiences of God's grace. This book will stimulate and energize your spirit toward a new embrace of the true meaning of the Christ experience."

—NINA GUNTER, general superintendent, Church of the Nazarene

"I never dreamed of the way in which a sustained discussion of anonymity could unlock so much spiritual wisdom. I hope this wonderful book inspires many to join the ranks of "God's secret agents"!"

—RICHARD MOUW, president, Fuller Theological Seminary

"From the time Jon and I first talked about this book, I have been unable to escape the good, hard, and serious issues it raises. As I take seriously Jon's instruction to live and act with deliberate avoidance of recognition or appreciation, with intentional anonymity, I am drawn by the Spirit to live intentionally in the presence of God, before whom I am never anonymous. I am profoundly grateful for this book."

—REUBEN WELCH, professor and author,
whose books include *We Really Do Need Each Other*

Signed,  Anonymous

Shedding the Need for Acknowledgment

Jon Johnston

BEACON HILL PRESS
OF KANSAS CITY

Copyright 2009
by Jon Johnston and Beacon Hill Press of Kansas City

ISBN 978-0-8341-2440-0

Printed in the United States of America

Cover Design: J.R. Caines
Interior Design: Sharon Page

All Scripture quotations not otherwise designated are from the *Holy Bible, New International Version*® (NIV®). Copyright © 1973, 1978, 1984 by International Bible Society. Used by permission of Zondervan Publishing House. All rights reserved.

Permission to quote from the following additional copyrighted versions of the Bible is acknowledged with appreciation:

The Living Bible (TLB), © 1971. Used by permission of Tyndale House Publishers, Inc., Wheaton, IL 60189. All rights reserved.

The Message (TM). Copyright © 1993, 1994, 1995, 1996, 2000, 2001, 2002. Used by permission of NavPress Publishing Group.

Scripture quotations marked KJV are from the King James Version of the Bible.

Library of Congress Cataloging-in-Publication Data

Johnston, Jon.
  Signed, anonymous : shedding the need for acknowledgment / Jon Johnston.
    p. cm.
  ISBN 978-0-8341-2440-0 (pbk.)
  1. Humility—Religious aspects—Christianity. 2. Service (Theology) I. Title.
BV4647.H8J64 2009
241'.4—dc22
                                                          2008055717

10 9 8 7 6 5 4 3 2 1

This book is dedicated to Cherry,
my beautiful and faithful wife,
who lovingly engages in quiet,
anonymous giving each day of her life.

Contents

Foreword, by Pat Boone	9
Introduction	15
Section 1: Worthy of Deep Reflection	
1. Giving Anonymity More than a Passing Glance	21
2. Neither Crowing nor Cowering	33
3. A Challenging Upstream Swim	45
Section 2: Wise Biblical Admonition	
4. Bright Light Shining from the Shadows	61
5. God's Ordinary People	77
6. Two Strategies, One Goal	89
Section 3: Wondrous Gateway to Immense Joy	
7. Adoration of the Father: Pure Worship	105
8. Heaven's Treasure Chest: Anticipated Reward	115
9. From Success to Significance: Authenticity	127
10. No More One-upmanship: True Identity	141
11. Capturing True Humility: Deflation	153
12. Witnessing with Pizzazz: Effective Transmission	163
13. Leaving the Best Legacy: Footprints	177
Conclusion	189

Foreword

This book deals with a neglected yet significant—even profound—subject. There is so much to be said on anonymity. It is so important to God, yet so poorly esteemed in our culture.

A story has circulated for some time about the fund-pledging event at a local synagogue. In the well-attended meeting, member after member of the congregation stood and spoke their names and the amount of money they were pledging to the current needs of the synagogue. A man stood and announced not just his name but also his place of business and its address, then concluded with "I pledge nine thousand dollars . . . *anonymous*." Well, not exactly.

It is difficult for human beings to do good things and expect absolutely no recognition. Perhaps you've seen the bumper sticker that admonishes "Practice random acts of kindness." That's almost biblical—as you'll soon see.

I've played at golf for 50 years and love it intensely. Playing in the various pro-celebrity tournaments on the West Coast, I often engaged the services of a good caddy named Ron. He had been recommended to me by Robert Goulet, saying he and his Vegas buddies nicknamed him "Ronnie the Rat." It was meant to be humorous.

When I met Ron and saw that he limped noticeably from an accident injury years before, I hesitated to even subject him to carrying my heavy bag and chasing my errant shots. Ron quickly assured me that this was the way he made his living, that his limp wasn't painful, and that he wanted the job. So for 10 years or more, Ronnie was my company, my caddie, and my friend on the golf course.

During those years I learned that he was an alcoholic and that the malady had robbed him of a career as an accountant, though he had a master's degree in economics. He was terribly hung-over some mornings, but he never missed a tee time, and he helped me on the golf course. There was a lot of time to talk and really get to know each other. I was able to share the Lord with him and at times pray with him about his problems. I really liked this fellow and felt real empathy for him. When he died, I felt as if I had lost a relative.

About a month later, a lawyer requested a meeting with me. He revealed he was settling Ron's affairs and that Ron had no living relatives. To my absolute astonishment, the lawyer explained to me that my former caddie and friend had left $35,000 in his will to The Pat Boone Foundation! Somewhere along the way, I had let him know that my wife, Shirley, and I had created a foundation through which we gave to the Lord and Christian causes but that it sounded more impressive than it was since only Shirley and I had made contributions to it. Now, unknown "Ronnie the Rat" had given to the Lord's work through our little-known foundation! He gave posthumously, which is about as anonymous as you can get.

Actually, it's rather hard to be *completely* anonymous in our good deeds. Eventually people seem to find out, and things like that are exceptionally interesting and impressive—perhaps because they seem so rare.

I'll never forget John L. Rainey, a man who taught Bible in the Christian high school I was fortunate to attend in Nashville. We kids had a field day joking about him and some of his peculiar traits. He was a large, corpulent man, with a perpetual five o'clock shadow on his jowls, and he always seemed to be sweating. He must have had a sense of humor somewhere, but he seemed to have misplaced it. In class he was all business, and the Bible is, after all, serious business.

His suits were shiny, his collars and cuffs frayed and soiled. We heard rumors that he was so stingy that he collected rainwater in pails to bathe and cook with and that he used only one light bulb at a time in his rundown house right across the street from our school. He often spoke in very simple aphorisms, like "Scholars, it's always right to do right; it's always wrong to do wrong." As you might imagine, we found those sayings funny.

But one day we were shocked to learn that Brother Rainey had passed away. Shortly thereafter we also learned that he had left *everything* in his bank account to our Christian school so that future generations of eager young kids could continue to be provided with knowledge of God's holy Word.

Suddenly we saw his "stinginess" in a different light. While old Brother Rainey spent very little on himself, he was "laying up treasures in heaven, where moth and rust would not corrupt, nor thieves break through to steal," as he had admonished in his classes. Sure, he could have announced his intentions in advance of his death and received accolades. But he chose to refrain from doing that.

To my knowledge, no building or room or anything else bears his name. In fact, most have forgotten his name or anything he did in this life. But be assured, he left an indelible impression on his students. He certainly did on me. And of infinitely more importance, his years of teaching and final gift are known to the Lord of all creation, and he has entered into what his Bible describes as "the joys of His Lord."

And that's the reason, I believe, for this wonderful book.

God himself is watching. He watches each of us, and His book says plainly He is Spirit—and He is *seeking* those who are born of the Spirit to worship Him "in spirit and in truth." (See John 4:24.) And though these words are eternally important and recorded for us by the Holy Spirit, they were spoken to a poor lost woman at the well in Samaria—spoken one-on-one to a woman who is still to this day is anonymous.

Also anonymous was the poor widow in Luke 21 who Jesus pointed out to His disciples as she dropped her two mites into the Temple collection box. I've thought of her so many times and marveled that the Son of the living God—himself God—noticed her and *knew that she was giving all she had.*

FOREWORD

She wasn't doing it to be noticed. She might well have been embarrassed that her gift was so pitifully small. But what so impacts me is that Jesus *did* notice, and though we'll never know her name, Jesus knew—and her deed has been recorded for all time, recorded where it truly counts—in His Book of Life and in His heart.

—Pat Boone

I Wonder

You know, Lord, how I serve You
With great emotional fervor
In the limelight.
You know how eagerly I speak for You
At a women's club
You know how I effervesce when I promote
A fellowship group.
You know my genuine enthusiasm
At a Bible study.
But how would I react, I wonder,
If You pointed to a basin of water
And asked me to wash the calloused feet
Of a bent and wrinkled old woman
Day after day
Month after month
In a room where nobody saw
And nobody knew?

—Ruth Harms Calkin

<www.preaching.com/resources>

Introduction

Some great truths sneak up on us like a skillful bandit; others suddenly jolt us like a smack on the side of the head. My appreciation for the freedom that comes from letting go of the need to be acknowledged impacted me *both* ways.

My first example of giving and expecting nothing in return was my father. I vividly recall his beneath-the-radar, anonymous acts of kindness. He had this thing about losing his clothing—frequently returning home without his socks or his coat. Put simply, Dad couldn't enjoy the comfort of his attire when others were in discomfort.

I can remember him standing beside my bed late at night, whispering a prayer for my well-being. He assumed I was asleep.

My heart has been warmed by many stories of folks who did things incognito for no other reason than an inner compulsion to do what's right.

While in the United States Senate, Oregon Senator Mark Hatfield often visited senators and representatives in Washington hospitals, regardless of political affiliation, to share a word of personal encouragement.

John Edward Caldwell, lifetime director of both Young Life and World Vision and a respected lawyer of 51 years, inconspicuously provided free legal advice to persons in dire need.

For decades Bill Stivers, my colleague at Pepperdine University, quietly taught Spanish to affluent residents of Malibu to finance an orphanage in Tijuana, Mexico.

A nameless Free Methodist minister's wife who randomly visited intensive care patients led my close relative to the Lord just moments before his passing.

Neither these folks nor the scores of others I've heard of or learned about are inclined to disclose their deeds of mercy. It was by happenstance that I learned of them.

But the "smack on my head" occurred when I studied the biblical account of our Lord's deeds and words. Jesus modeled and straightforwardly expressed His strong preference for devotion expressed in secret—the kind that solicits not even a tincture of earthly acclaim, devotion generated from obedient, holy, and generous hearts—hearts desiring to please God alone.

Immediately after receiving this brain thump, I scrambled to locate sources to shed light on my discovery. Amazingly, though often alluded to in both the Old and New Testaments, I discovered that there is a scarcity of books or articles on the theme. Furthermore, I couldn't recall hearing a single sermon on the subject.

Could this glaring oversight be intentional? Drowned out by a culture that incessantly pushes us to toot our own horns, this runs crossgrain to human nature. It was then that I began sensing a strong compulsion to explore this crucial but neglected topic. Since my primary investigation uncovered nothing in literature, I decided to simply ask people about anonymous living and giving.

I distributed nearly 300 questionnaires to a wide assortment of people ranging from biblical scholars to faithful laypeople. I asked questions such as *Have you ever seriously considered walking this pathway? Have you been impacted by others who have?*

The replies astounded me. Most contained several pages of profound insights and touching illustrations. Unexpectedly, more than a few strongly encouraged me in my pursuit, hoping to gain personal guidance from my book. I was convinced that I had touched a nerve.

With the inspiration of God's Spirit and the affirmation of so many, I couldn't resist the temptation to begin recording and organizing my thoughts. The culmination of that joyful effort is in your hands.

Please don't consider my work any sort of final word or authority on this subject. Nor should you consider me someone who practices and embodies all I know to be true. I've simply embarked on a rewarding journey, and I invite you to join me. It's a journey fraught with challenges. But make no mistake—it's one that offers incalculable rewards.

Let us begin thinking of ourselves as God's agents of inconspicuous, humble service. Pursuing this course is sure to impact others in a redemptive way, because we'll bring glory to the ultimate example of loving, anonymous giving.

Our low-profile deeds of worship will not be ignored by the one whose glory we promote. Jesus emphatically promised, "Your Father, who sees what is done in secret, will reward you" (Matthew 6:18). And deep down, isn't that the recognition we most desire?

Section One

Worthy of Deep Reflection

One
Giving Anonymity More than a Passing Glance

A huge mystery has been solved in Kansas City. The true identity of the metropolitan area's "Secret Santa" has been disclosed. For a span of 26 years this person anonymously roamed the streets each December and dispersed a total of $1.3 million to ecstatic, mostly underprivileged, recipients.

In the final year of his life, after being diagnosed with incurable esophageal cancer, Larry Stewart confessed to being the Secret Santa. According to him, his purpose was to inspire others to do similar random acts of kindness. In his simple words, "That's what we're here for, to help other people."

He made his millions in cable TV and long-distance telephone service. His private holiday giving began in December 1979, when he was at a drive-in restaurant nursing his wounds after being fired. Actually, it was the second year in a row he lost his job the week before Christmas.

"It was cold, and this carhop didn't have on a very big jacket," he tells. "And I said to myself: *I think I got it bad? She's out in this cold making nickels and dimes.*" He gave her a $20 bill and told her to keep the change.

Seeing her grateful response and feeling a deep inner satisfaction, he was motivated thereafter to joyfully dispense yuletide monetary happiness. Often it was in $100 bills—sometimes two or three at a time. Best of all, he did it anonymously. He wasn't working an angle for profit. There was no display to attract the media spotlight—just plain, unadulterated benevolence straight from his warm and grateful heart.

Why was Kansas City's attention galvanized on this mystery person for more than a quarter of a century? Primarily it was because Larry Stewart chose to give anonymously—which required careful planning, tremendous resolve, and a big dose of humility. He didn't desire thunderous applause or a front-page splash in the *Kansas City Star.*

When his identity was finally revealed due to his terminal illness, it created a mini-revolution of praise and admiration. That's because Larry Stewart connected people with one of humanity's finer attributes—sharing with those who are in need.

It's not uncommon to share with those to whom we're committed, such as family. But he awakened an awareness of sharing with complete strangers and did so as a matter of course, *not* because it was likely to enhance his reputation or result in a big financial windfall.

Just for Kicks

Something else struck me about this story: Larry Stewart never made any reference to being prompted by Christian faith—no response to a minister's appeal, no attempt to score points with God.

Although unintentionally adhering to a definite biblical admonition more closely than many believers I know, Mr. Stewart's benevolence was probably based on these three nonreligious motivations:

1. An inner compulsion for doing the right thing
2. Gratitude for coming into riches
3. Good feelings he received from seeing others happy.

Commendable. But come to think of it, the Secret Santa's benevolence might not be quite as rare as we think. Many persons, similarly motivated, come to mind.

A close friend of the late Elvis Presley revealed that the wealthy musician gave away 21 new Cadillacs during his lifetime. As far as anyone knows, *none* of the recipients had a clue who had gifted them. Furthermore, apparently no religious intent was involved.

It was the King of Rock and Roll's style to hang out near a Memphis dealer's showroom until a deserving-looking couple came along. He would see them ogle a shiny new luxury car with that sure-would-be-nice-but-there's-no-way look in their eyes. They would paw the massive grill, closely examine the panorama of dashboard buttons, even start the engine to hear it roar—lingering to dream as long as possible.

After determining from his safe distance which vehicle was the couple's favorite, the singer would sneak through a rear entrance to the dealer's business office and write a check for the car. Then Elvis would rush out, and again at a safe distance, watch with satisfaction as the salesperson explained it to the ecstatic but mystified owners of a brand-new Cadillac.

Larry Stewart and Elvis repeated their costly gestures simply to see others happy. But neither of them was making a concerted attempt to fulfill a biblical mandate.

Many years ago television featured a series titled *The Millionaire*. Although a million bucks still doesn't exactly seem like chickenfeed today, at the time this television show was on the air, a million dollars was a vast, almost incomprehensible fortune.

Each episode began with the portrayal of a person or family victimized by a huge financial crisis. Such persons were severely destitute with no solutions in sight. To further intensify their distress, bill collectors hounded them relentlessly for immediate payment. Their lives were miserable and hopeless.

Then came the good part. A distinguished-looking man clutching a fancy briefcase knocked on the front door of a humble dwelling. When the person opened the door, the man would briefly declare something like "An anonymous donor has singled you out to receive one million dollars in cash with absolutely no strings attached. All that is required of you is to accept the satchel I am holding, filled with that amount of money. Please don't thank me; I am merely the delivery person for a generous donor whose only desire is to make you happy."

Following the recipient's look of extreme shock were screams of delight and tears of joy often followed by a brief period of stunned silence.

The man quickly and quietly turned and departed. The storyline then drifted into the ways this monetary gift made a positive impact on the lives of the recipients. I recall that each episode allowed viewers to vicariously enjoy their pleasure.

After examining these admirable deeds, we're left to wonder, *How could such anonymous generosity occur without an overpowering religious motivation?* Is it an attempt to please or impress God or gain inner assurance of adhering to a biblical teaching?

The simple fact is that we're all created in the image of God. (See Genesis 1:26-27.) Regardless of who we are or what we do, a residue of our Heavenly Father's image is embedded in us.

Briefly put, humanity is hard-wired with a propensity to do good deeds. Admittedly, benevolence is often narrowly channeled, as when ruthless Mafioso godfathers gush with affection as they lavish gifts on their deeply loved grandchildren.

Bottom line: due to our God-given nature, even generosity for generosity's sake bathes the human spirit in blessing. My father often said, "It's impossible to sprinkle the perfume of happiness onto someone else without spilling a big dose of it on yourself." And for some strange reason, we just seem to spill more onto ourselves when we sprinkle it onto others anonymously.

If anonymity is so important, it deserves our careful scrutiny. With this in mind, let's take a closer look at its nature and implications.

A Lot More than Bucks

Giving anonymously, as meritorious as it may seem, includes more than just handing out money in a spectacular display of generosity. That's because we humans are provided with far more than money and what we can purchase. We've all been allocated three additional, critically important resources: time, energy, and special talents.

We determine, based on our priorities, just how these resources will be deployed. They can be squandered, used selfishly, or dedicated to purposes that align with Christian servanthood. It's our call.

I would venture to say that for most of us a fairly sizeable slice of our lives includes some sort of anonymous giving that involves time, energy, and special talents—plus money—especially to people and purposes we love. Furthermore, we resist thinking of ourselves as martyrs. In fact, it seems as though we're far more likely to consider ourselves privileged.

Let's examine a few life situations, occupations, and roles that include sizeable numbers of anonymous givers—folks who are likely to dispense their time, energy, and personal talents in quiet giving.

There's no clamor for notoriety from the wife and mother who repeatedly engages in the thankless three Ds—dusting, diaper-changing, and dish-washing. She includes these daily tasks in her busy life without alerting family members that they were done. The same is true of the husband and father who goes to work, helps his children with homework, and maintains the yard. No big celebrations are expected, no special awards or citations.

Add ministers to the list. I'm reminded of one whose story touched my heart. My friend Marty Butler arrived at church early for a convention to find the pastor vacuuming the foyer. At the last minute the custodian had called in sick, and this man of the cloth was making sure the building was ready for company. He had hoped to finish before anyone arrived so no one would think badly of the custodian, and he wanted no credit.

Let's add caregivers too. These folks faithfully respond to the continuous and demanding needs of the sick and debilitated. According to a recent *Newsweek* article, more than 20 million American households contain persons who look after loved ones.

Caregiving can extract a heavy toll. Admittedly, it can also offer positive results: personal fulfillment, a guiltless future, a feeling of giving back. But research increasingly links it to negative health trends, such as weakened immunity, depression, and premature death caused by the increased stress.

Another extremely noteworthy group is one I term "bridge people." These are faithful pilgrims who are content to connect persons in need with those who can meet their needs. They are content with others receiving the credit, realizing that what they do is essential in making redemptive connections.

Who better exemplifies bridge people than Holocaust sympathizers who secretly arranged for the safety and eventual escape of Jewish people? In spite of Adolph Hitler's threats of severe punishment, they stubbornly refused to cease and desist. These courageous heroes had one major goal: matching those who desperately needed help with ones who were eager and able to provide it. For obvious reasons, they were content to remain anonymous. Their commendable deeds were sufficient to provide them with ample reward.

I've predominantly mentioned persons whose identities are either unknown, who are blended with like-minded persons such as moms and wives, or who are discovered much later due to special circumstances, such as the Secret Santa.

Yes, we've extolled anonymity, but it should not be deified in our thinking. Anonymity isn't always commendable, honorable, or a sign of taking the high ground. In truth, it's often aligned with sinister motives and completely sordid goals.

Anonymity Gone Haywire

I heard the story recently of an unidentified donor who dropped in on a nearby Christian institution of higher learning and unexpectedly plunked down a gift of $75 million.

To this cash-strapped school, it was like manna from heaven. The school's intense financial worries were a thing of the past. No more drawn-out fundraising campaigns to suffer through. Everyone could look to the future and construct long lists of heretofore unrealistic expenditures.

The celebration was long and loud. But then the real truth was exposed. The secret donor actually had his eye set on rezoning the land that completely encircled the campus in order to initiate an extremely profitable real estate development. He figured that he had purchased the school's support and could count on them when the controversial issue was voted on by the city fathers.

And that's not all. Further investigation revealed that his fortune had originated from his wife's inheritance. That in itself is not blameworthy—except for the fact that her parents had made their fortune through ties to the Las Vegas mafia.

Here is someone who hid behind anonymity to work a shady, lucrative deal. Anonymity did nothing to purge the fact that a very suspect deal was in the works.

I've not heard how the whole scenario played out, but with God's guidance and grace, I'm hopeful that these well-intentioned persons are not spiritually impaired nor their reputable institution morally stained.

The point is that anonymous living and giving aren't always morally pure or spiritually commendable. Following are instances when anonymity hides weakness or evil.

Anonymity is used as a means of hiding after being hurt. One grieves and withdraws instead of getting back in the batter's box and inviting life's next pitch.

Anonymity is used to conceal one's true self, so that one becomes deceitfully nontransparent. One becomes an impostor, playing a fictitious role. This most often occurs when one feels threatened or fearful or suffers from a negative self-concept.

Anonymity is a fictitious ploy secretly hoping to be revealed; the person may even leak information of the feigned anonymous acts to gain praise. This is especially insidious because it involves mimicking the authentic in order to obtain plaudits. It indicates a condition of intense desperation.

Anonymity is used to snoop, intimidate, or stalk in order to reach some goal. Persons targeted in this way are driven batty when anonymity is used to intrude into another's business or private life.

Anonymity is a cover for cowardice. Anonymous love notes are common and excused in elementary school. Adults, however, sometimes resort to sending anonymous letters because they fear repercussions. Such cowardly tidings are characteristically irresponsible and often quite cruel in tone.

What is the common thread that connects all of these? What essential factor tarnishes the use of anonymity? It really all comes down to motive.

The M Word—Motive

In the secular world, motive counts for a ton. Whenever a child does something irresponsible, a parent quickly asks himself or herself if the child *meant* to do it. Typically, a careless spill results in admonishment. An ill-intentioned behavior such as stealing earns rebuke and stern discipline. The first is deemed accidental or even reckless; the second is seen as sinister or sinful. It's about the motive.

Where is motive more important than in a court of law? In capital cases, for instance, intention—as evidenced by premeditation—can be the difference between the death penalty and life imprisonment.

Undeniably, motive is considered vitally important in most aspects of living. But far more so, it's crucial in regard to acceptably serving our Lord. Who better substantiates this than the psalmist?

He invites the intense scrutiny of the Divine—starting with motive—when declaring: "Search me, O God, and know my heart; test me and know my anxious thoughts. See if there is any offensive way in me, and lead me in the way everlasting" (Psalm 139:23-24).

So how do we square our motives with actions? We can be guilty of wrong action with the wrong motive, right action with the wrong motive, and other motive and action combinations. Pairing the right action rooted in the right motive should be our goal.

If we fail to attain the goal of right action and right motive, it's important to know that motive always trumps action. T. S. Eliot said "the greatest treason" is "to do the right thing for the wrong reason."

Why is motive primary? It's because improving action can be taught and learned, but improving motive requires a transformation of being. A divinely cleansed heart results in a deep desire to truly do His will.

Even more intensely, we desire His revolutionizing presence so that we can proclaim with the psalmist, "As the deer pants for streams of water, so my soul pants for you, O God" (Psalm 42:1).

Bonding with our Heavenly Abba is certain to result in authentic peace and power in our lives. And it's certainly not because of anything we vow, create, or offer Him. Our marvelous transformation is *because* of Him. To paraphrase the late, greatly loved minister Adrian Rogers, we resemble a nuclear plant. Lacking the ability to generate power, we are able only to release it.

What causes us to live and give secretly without a trace of doing so for acclaim or reward? Giving with a pure motive that only the Lord can create within us.

Such a life yields authentic joy.

Discussion Questions

1. Have you ever heard about or encountered someone whose secret generosity was accidentally discovered? What positives resulted?

2. In your opinion, why do people—quite apart from any religious reasons—engage in anonymous acts of generosity or compassion?

3. Share any stories about folks you've known or heard about who operate anonymously but have motives that seem very suspect.

4. Do you know of people who receive little or no recognition or encouragement, even though others know of them, such as parents, caregivers, or bridge-people?

5. When it comes to your personal allotment of money, time, energy, and gifts, is it your desire to devote more to anonymous living? If so, what are likely to be your highest hurdles to get over?

Action Items

1. Ask God for guidance, and then—no matter how seemingly insignificant—attempt to do something good anonymously. Try doing good without expecting to see a return on your investment.

2. Try to become aware of persons who give to your world anonymously. If possible, express appreciation or offer encouragement to at least one of them.

Two
Neither Crowing nor Cowering

George Lyons, my friend and a theologian, related an inspiring story. While doing his doctoral studies, he met David, a man he calls the kindest person he ever met.

When David was 18 and fresh out of high school, he worked at a nursing home before heading to nurse's training. David met a young man there, a quadriplegic with no family. He promised the young man he would write him every month after going away to school. He faithfully did so during nurse's training and a subsequent military career, and he continued to write to the man until his death.

David's last name was Killem. As a young nurse, he was very troubled by the reaction of the patients when he was paged over the loudspeaker: "Nurse Killem." To allay fears, he went through considerable red tape to legally change his name to Clark, his mother's maiden name.

At one point David worked for public health. On his own time he methodically tracked down skid-row transients to make certain they had received their tuberculosis shots. Though unheralded, this action doubtlessly saved many lives.

David never took life easy; he considered himself on duty even when driving down the street in his car. He carried a saw and hedge trimmer in his trunk. When approaching an intersection where there was foliage obstructing a stop sign, he would stop, trim the branches, and place the discards in his trunk. He was too concerned about the wellbeing of others to ignore a safety hazard.

David kept a list of birthdays and anniversaries of every member of his large church in Atlanta. On each person's birthday, he called and played "Happy Birthday" on his flute over the phone. He also played flute in a group that visited nursing homes in the city.

David worked for years for an Atlanta florist on holidays, delivering flowers for one reason—so regular employees could spend that day with their families. It was just another way he sprinkled kindness.

According to George, these accounts of David's kindnesses are just the tip of the iceberg. Most impressive of all, David never crowed about any of his sacrificial and compassionate gestures. He just kept on keeping on, constantly and consistently engaged in thoughtful, loving service. When he died recently, in his 90s, many people came to his funeral to testify to his remarkable legacy.

Another Song in a Minor Key

Contrast George's friend David with someone Charles Swindoll once described. In Lincoln, Kansas, stands a bizarre collection of elaborate gravestones erected by farmer John Davis.

Mr. Davis started out as a hired hand, but by sheer determination and penny-pinching, he amassed a huge fortune. Unfortunately, in the process he made few friends. He remained especially distant from his wife's family, who believed their daughter had married far beneath her dignity. Sensing this, an embittered John vowed never to leave his in-laws one thin dime.

When his wife died, he built an elaborate statue to her memory. A sculptor was hired to design the monument, depicting the two of them sitting at opposite ends on a love seat. Pleased with the result, John commissioned a second statue of himself kneeling and placing a wreath upon her grave.

Considering himself on a roll, he ordered a third monument depicting his wife kneeling at *his* future gravesite, again, depositing a wreath. Then, with cost being no concern, he instructed the sculptor to add a pair of wings on her back to make her look angelic.

Incredibly, Mr. Davis plunked down a cool quarter-million for these monuments. Realizing that he was frittering away big bucks, some city leaders entreated him to donate to legitimate community projects—hospital equipment, park land, a children's pool. But the old miser frowned and cynically muttered, "Not on your life! What's this town ever done for me? I owe it nothin'!"

That's not the end of the story. After depleting his resources on statuary, John Davis became a grim-faced resident of the poorhouse. Then, like David Clark, he passed away in his 90s. What about the monuments? Ironically, they began to sink into the Kansas soil, rapidly succumbing to the ravages of time, vandalism, and neglect. Within a few years these sad reminders of a self-centered life will completely vanish.

Unlike David Clark's funeral, few attended John's funeral; and those who came didn't seem remorseful. There was, however, one exception. One fellow was genuinely gripped by a sense of personal loss—none other than Horace England, the prosperous tombstone salesman.

John's and David's lives are light-years apart in important ways. David Clark lost himself in a continuous stream of kind and thoughtful actions. John Davis poured his money, time, energy, and talents into monuments of vanity. David Clark shied away from parading himself or his kind works; John Davis devoted himself to displaying lavish—and pretty goofy—identity footprints.

Result? Mr. Clark's compassionate heart and the hearts of those he impacted were saturated with joy. Mr. Davis's selfish heart became increasingly tormented with intense bitterness.

SECTION 1

Getting a Whiff of Pride

A simple but true ancient adage proclaims, "Self-praise smells bad." To again paraphrase Charles Swindoll, it doesn't matter how we prepare it, garnish it with extras, or serve it on our finest china—its pungent odor remains. No seasoning can eliminate the offensive reek. And, like spoiled meat, aging only putrefies it more!

In sharp contrast, the author of the second letter to the Corinthians declares that lives praising God exude the opposite aroma: "Everywhere we go, people breathe in the exquisite fragrance. Because of Christ, we give off a sweet scent rising to God, which is recognized by those on the way of salvation—an aroma redolent with life" (2 Corinthians 2:14-15, TM).

It all comes down to the *target* of our praise. God's Word waves plenty of red flags to dissuade us from pursuing this course. The Book of Proverbs repeatedly conveys our Heavenly Father's opinion on arrogance. Pulling no punches, it declares that He detests haughty eyes (Proverbs 6:17) and bluntly labels a proud heart "sin" (Proverbs 21:4). Put simply, any praise we receive must not be self-generated. "Let another praise you, and not your own mouth" (Proverbs 27:2).

We must shun the temptation to be our own cheerleaders. This could be why our Heavenly Father designed our arms so that it's terribly difficult for us to reach around far enough to pat ourselves on the back!

The apostle Paul trumpets the identical message, spotlighting self-deception: "If anyone thinks he is something when he is nothing, he deceives himself" (Galatians 6:3). The point is clear. Apart from our Lord, we're nothing. Conning ourselves into thinking otherwise produces only foul-smelling odors in our lives, such as false security, ingratitude, and abrasiveness.

Why is David Clark's example relevant to us today? Most of us are prone to construct monuments of vanity—not the marble kind but ones even more blatantly designed to provide platforms for self-praise. Examples include amassing fortune ("dying with the most toys"), amassing fame ("making the tabloids"), amassing power (being known as a "mover and shaker"), and amassing pleasure ("going for all the gusto").

All of these focus squarely on *getting*. By comparison, the message of our Lord zeros in on becoming eternally rich through *giving*—serving others rather than leaving footprints on their backs, surrendering rights rather than becoming control freaks, saying, "No," when our flesh clamors for us to shout, "Yes!"

Our Lord's entire package of instruction is wrapped up in one simple statement: "Seek first his kingdom and his righteousness, and all these things will be given to you as well" (Matthew 6:33). Psychologists call it "delayed gratification"—investing in the present in order to receive rich dividends in the future.

Let's take a quick glance at the life of Jesus. Granted, others commemorate it with ostentatious memorials. The most striking I've seen is that which surrounds the supposed location of His cross inside Jerusalem's Church of the Holy Sepulcher. Here is an incredible display of gilded crosses, bejeweled statues, and ornaments of all descriptions. But we must clearly understand that our Lord's tastes were exceedingly simple—which coincided with His humble Spirit. Thus, it's not surprising that He never left—nor ordered us to construct—gaudy shrines or ridiculous marble monstrosities.

Instead, Jesus fixed His resolute eyes on one purpose: pursuing a life of righteousness in perfect conformity with the will of His Father. And He lived that life to the max—pulling out all the stops. Absolutely nothing was held back.

May we aspire to do the same, as our gracious Savior provides us the grace and strength.

Unlikely Strut and Swagger

We can likely agree that most persons who quietly do good under the radar tend to do so for reasons other than arrogance. Such persons are probably not obsessed with a compulsion to inflate their own egos.

They are more inclined to play second fiddle, which, according to famed conductor Leonard Bernstein, is the hardest instrument to play in a symphony orchestra.

It's also reasonable to assume that under-the-radar servants are unaccustomed to receiving attention; they're more likely to be taken for granted. But for them it's not a big deal, and certainly no reason to indulge in self-pity or retaliation.

They're just grateful for the opportunity to serve, hoping their service will relieve the burdens of others and produce tangible blessings. They're content to let others receive applause and take bows.

Their motivation is to be obedient to the Master they adore, and they long to someday hear Him say,

> Well done, good and faithful servant; thou hast been faithful over a few things, I will make thee ruler over many things: enter thou into the joy of thy Lord" *(Matthew 25:23, KJV).*

There is, however, a caveat. Though definitely not driven by the need for credit on earth, I can't help but wonder how inconspicuous servants keep their cool when encountering impostors—persons who cleverly solicit and accept undeserved acclaim.

An editor friend of mine shared a story about someone she knows and deeply cares for; we'll call her Sally. Sally is consumed by the responsibilities and accompanying stresses related to caring for her aging and dying mother.

Remarkably, her mother manages to attend church quite frequently. When at church, she typically chooses to sit beside the caregiver's brother and sister-in-law. When church is over, people often approach Sally and declare something such as "It's truly remarkable how your brother and sister-in-law help you with your mother's care. I'm sure you couldn't make it without their help."

This causes Sally to start wondering, *Are my brother and his wife lying and deceiving these people? Why do they stand there and remain silent and bask in undeserved praise?*

They have to know that sitting next to Sally's mother in church for barely an hour doesn't remotely compare to shouldering the heavy load 99.9 percent of the time.

Knowing Sally intimately, my editor friend strongly doubts that Sally is craving credit. Instead, it's her impression that Sally tenderly serves her mother strictly out of love and familial duty. But the fact remains that hearing others get credit and accepting it makes her blood boil. Why? Because a misperception is being allowed to persist.

Calling attention to themselves is usually the last thing caregivers are tempted to do. For them, remaining in the shadows is just fine. Being praised by others is light years away from what they're all about.

Most anonymous givers aren't fans of self-promotion, but they're not proponents of self-depreciation. Nor should they be. As a rule, we won't find them walking around with martyr's complex or considering themselves victims. Most realize that this, ironically, would be a blatant display of pride.

Muted Adulation Without Flagellation

God's agents are not given to crowing or cowering. Cowering implies diminishing ourselves because we feel insecure or unworthy. It's helpful to think of it as the opposite of strutting and swaggering.

Those who live and give anonymously, whether simply or grandiosely, are mostly people to be admired. The sheer fact of choosing to give without fanfare is noteworthy and sets such persons apart. But ones who are motivated by love and the burning desire to please their Lord qualify as bona fide heroes to emulate.

It seemed providential that just today I learned of the simple anonymous gesture of a Christian servant. Although definitely not large on the radar screen of magnanimous deeds, in my mind it certainly qualifies as very significant. See if you agree.

SECTION 1

One of the students at the university where I teach entered the laundry room in his dorm and discovered that another student had left clothes in the dryer. Needing to use the dryer himself, he realized that he would need to remove these articles to make room for his own.

Instead of tossing the other guy's clothes onto a chair in a wrinkled heap, he took the time to neatly fold each piece, concluding that doing so was consistent with the values he professed to embrace as a Christian. When finished, he carefully placed the stack of clothes onto a table. Please keep in mind that nobody saw him do this, and he had no clue as to whose clothes they were.

While explaining, he assured me that he didn't give much thought to the incident, which is typical of his kind of people. Then he continued with the story. A couple of weeks later, he happened to return to get his clothes from the dryer a bit late. He was startled to see a fellow standing there folding *his* clothes. With a smile he said, "Thanks, dude."

The guy looked up and replied, "I'm really glad to be doing this. A couple of weeks ago I was late getting back for my clothes, and some really nice person did this for me. I felt so good about it that I decided that if I ever had the chance, I'd do it for someone else."

I explained to the young man that he had experienced firsthand the ripple and the boomerang effects of kindness. His example had no doubt been observed and discussed by several. Furthermore, it prompted at least one to repeat the deed—a kind gesture that happened to return kindness to him. This young man is a sower of good seed that germinated and bore fruit. (See Matthew 13:3-9.)

This student's anonymous act of thoughtfulness yielded tangible good. When he realized this and shared his story with me, there was no display on his part of cockiness or braggadocio. But neither did he cower by saying things such as anyone would have done what he did or that the other guy probably would have folded his clothes anyway.

There was no false humility or insistence that he should receive no credit. This young man shared his story so that we could both rejoice. Hopefully, he will be encouraged to launch more acts of anonymous kindnesses. I know his story encouraged me to do the same.

The Hidden Revealed

Most anonymous givers are reticent to share their secret good deeds. For them, crowing does not compute. Like the mother of our Lord, they have a marvelous capacity for harboring things in their hearts (Luke 2:19).

As we've stated, anonymous givers are better suited than most to perform good deeds in the shadows. Still, their very humanity must prompt them at times to desire for others to know and care, to feel appreciated, to receive some assurance that they're making a difference. But when others have no knowledge of their deeds, feelings of isolation and insulation can produce negative effects that can eventually lead to something that looks like cowering.

So what does this mean? It implies that the rest of us have a crucial part to play in their lives. We can—with wisdom and discretion—help make the invisible visible. Their inspirational stories can be shared. In so doing, we can encourage them to hold their heads a little higher or at least droop into self-depreciation.

Several kinds of recognition have been instituted to commend those who do good deeds below the radar. They have many labels, and not all are tied to religious organizations. Here are some I'm aware of are:

- Service Above Self Award, Rotary Clubs International
- Caught in the Act, Kingswood Senior Home, Kansas City
- Secret Encouragers, Chinese Community Church, San Diego
- Service in the Shadows, Kansas City District, Church of the Nazarene
- Acts of Kindness. Refer to <www.actsofkindness.org>.

Author and sociologist David Moberg has a way with words. In responding to my survey, he succinctly declares, "Often the servants . . . with non-praised spiritual gifts are the ones who most need encouragement to continue behind-the-scenes good works that contribute significantly to the fruitfulness of the Body of Christ." (See 1 Corinthians 12:22-23.)

I believe we should showcase them often. Such persons realize deep down that they will never solicit such recognition, so when it's freely offered to them in respect and gratitude, their spirits are boosted, and their motivation is refueled. In no way is this an attempt to declare them celebrities or inflate their egos. Instead, it is to declare them heroes whose examples we should emulate.

No crowing. No cowering. The right place is somewhere in between.

Discussion Questions

1. Which of David Clark's gestures of kindness impressed you the most? Why?

2. In what ways have you found pride to produce a foul odor? Are there any conditions under which it smells pleasant?

3. Of the four monuments of vanity mentioned—amassing fortune, amassing fame, amassing power, amassing pleasure—which one seems to be the most prevalent?

4. Have you ever known anyone who solicited self-praise by cowering? Share.

5. What does in-between crowing and cowering look like to you?

Action Items:

1. Go to someone who faithfully and cheerfully plays second fiddle and offer words of genuine encouragement. Or better yet, reward him or her in a tangible way.

2. Try doing a good deed anonymously for someone you don't know. Monitor whether any ripple or boomerang effect transpires.

Three
A Challenging Upstream Swim

An arrogant frog lived in a pond. He considered himself much smarter than any of his peers. He often watched Canada geese fly overhead and occasionally chatted with the geese that landed on the water, impressing them with his intellect.

One day the little green genius came up with a scheme. On the next landing of geese, he sidled up to the most stalwart and explained that he admired his ability to fly to breathtaking heights. Also, he admitted that he had often dreamed of experiencing that firsthand.

Then he disclosed his plan: "If I put my mouth around your leg, I could hold on, go up with you, and see the glorious sights you see. I don't weigh much, and my bite won't hurt at all."

The goose cordially replied, "It's fine with me."

The bird readied to fly. The frog said his goodbyes, clamped his mouth on the goose's leg, and up they soared.

As they gained altitude, a person about a mile away from the pond looked up and saw something hanging from one of the geese. He pointed it out to his friend nearby, declaring, "There's a frog that has taken hold of that goose's leg and is going along for a ride. I wonder who thought of that."

The frog heard the person, and bursting with pride just couldn't resist answering, "I did!" You know what happened next.

This miniature amphibian engaged in self-promotion to his unfortunate demise. Likewise, we've all witnessed people pushing themselves forward, pulling strings, climbing and manipulating to gain recognition. One-upmanship seems basic to our nature and may even edge out baseball as America's number-one pastime.

Commanding Center Stage

Like the frog, most of us hunger for recognition. Not content with the proverbial 15 minutes of fame we're all supposed to get before we die, many of us crave the spotlight for as long as possible. Our egos are super-sized.

If successful, many of us become swaggeringly ostentatious, while others boast in subtle ways. But either way, the message is "Look at me!" On the other hand, when our track record is unimpressive, we often manipulate people into believing we're something that we aren't. You might say that if we have it, we flaunt it, and if we don't have it, we fake it.

Whether intentional or not, we inadvertently impart this message to our children. No wonder the current crop has been tagged the "trophy generation." As one child development expert puts it, kids today feel entitled to be rewarded even for lackluster performance.

Not long ago I was in a restaurant where Little Leaguers were receiving extravagant trophies at an awards ceremony. I turned to the leader and said, "Congratulations! It looks like you won the championship." She promptly assured me her team had come in a distant fourth! But nonetheless, it was still trophy time. Hungry egos must be fed.

This created fantasy principle was underscored in a recent study of third-graders from 14 nations. They were asked where they thought their country's kids ranked in math and science. Results? American children assessed it was a slam dunk—first in both categories. By contrast, South Korean children surmised that they would rank dead last!

Exams were administered and results tallied. The American kids came in a dismal 14, while the South Korean youngsters topped all other nations. Possessing self-confidence was not sufficient to insure high-quality performance. Arguably, it may have inhibited it.

This is not to say that self-respect and self-confidence are unimportant. Jesus clearly admonished us to love our neighbor as ourselves. (See Matthew 22:39.) Not more, not less, but *as* ourselves. Still, we must not allow self-love to lapse into obnoxious, counterproductive arrogance. The latter inevitably wreaks irreparable damage to the psyche and eventually impedes performance.

Push Inevitably Becomes Shove

No doubt about it—our culture is intrusive. We are prone to absorb surrounding influences like sponges. Realizing this, Paul cautions: "Don't let the world squeeze you into its mold" (Romans 12:2, TLB). If we're to avoid being conquered by the culture, we must seriously cue in on the nature of its intrusions.

Despite its many assets, our culture compels us to use achievements—real or imagined—for self-promotion. Why? It maintains that through this gateway we can best fulfill our desires and dreams. After all, if we don't promote ourselves, who will?

Self-promotion is a firmly entrenched cultural norm, a persisting standard that guides behavior, attitude, and thought and is woven into the fabric of our culture. If we're resistant to showcasing ourselves, we appear to be abnormal.

Our culture insists that—

We must stand out. The squeaky wheel gets the grease. This philosophy sharply contrasts with that of the typical Asian culture—namely, the nail that sticks out gets pounded.

We must purposely command attention. We must give the world good reason to shine the spotlight on us by initiating, achieving, asserting. In short, like a spoiled child, we must clamor for attention.

The kind of attention we draw is optional. Attention-getting strategies can yield negative as well as positive results. Our culture maintains that bad publicity is far preferable to getting no publicity at all.

What we believe we are—or others believe we are—is more important than who we really are. The postmodernist view is that one's perspective is what matters. Forget truth and reality—those are just illusions. Given this perspective, we're advised to visualize anything that aligns with our goals, interests, and wishes.

For celebrities, it's all or nothing. Either the star of fame is burning brightly, or it's extinguished. In other words, you're either hot or you're not; you're either idolized or trashed.

Once the downward slide begins, it often gains speed. In her latter years, film star Joan Crawford's reality jolt came while awaiting an elevator. She overheard a woman standing behind her say to a friend, "See that old woman there? She *used to be* Joan Crawford."

Most Christians aren't celebrities, nor do we aspire to be. We're just plain folks who go to work, barbeque on Memorial Day, try to not make enemies, and desire to faithfully serve our Lord.

This Mirror Doesn't Lie

In spite of our ordinariness, many of us are just as susceptible to craving admiration as those who live in the spotlight. In short, when it comes to self-promotion, we may be more similar to celebrities than different.

God's Word declares that "Man looks on the outward appearance" (1 Samuel 16:7). Our culture takes this to extremes. Consider the wide range of cosmetic surgeries, hair extensions, expensive tattoos, designer clothes, and jewelry that even teenagers and some children desire. Our culture is obsessed with how we look; we deeply desire to favorably impress.

In addition to appearance, our culture touts individual achievement. Consider key ways we measure worth: grade-point averages (GPA), credit scores, batting average, Medals of Honor, Oscars, Olympic medals. In each case, acclaim is bestowed on single individuals—not families, clubs, associations, or groups. Group awards exist, of course, but they seem of less importance.

We showcase *personal* achievements. Wishing others to know of our accomplishments, we parade them. Notice the small child who builds a sandcastle at the beach and yells, "Hey, Mom and Dad—look what I did!" Or note the executive who covers his office wall with award plaques. In both instances, primary attention is on individual merit.

I'm amused when an athlete repeatedly tells sportscasters that, hands down, team success is really what matters. Yeah, right! The athlete's helmet displays stick-on symbols that show the number of outstanding plays attributed to him or her as an individual. Is team success considered important? To a degree. But I contend that personal accomplishment weighs far more.

Contrast this scenario with a facsimile Olympics held recently on a Navaho Indian reservation. There were impressive-looking trophies displayed, and the Native American participants were urged to win them by running the fastest.

The starting pistol fired for the most important long-distance event. One obviously superior youth shot to the front as track officials cheered him on. As he began the last lap, to their astonishment, he began to slow his pace, glancing back at the other runners. He wasn't winded; nevertheless, he continued lessening his speed. Near the finish line, several other runners caught up with him, and the entire group broke the tape together.

The event organizers, a tad angry and disappointed, ran up to him and began asking why he blew the race. He would now have to share the trophy! With a big smile and without batting an eye he declared, "Out here we're happiest when we win together."

In those few words, this stalwart lad had vividly revealed the sharp contrast between two cultures. One features fierce individualistic competition and achievement; the other embraces group cooperation resulting in solidarity and unanimity.

The audience of culture judges us with certain criteria in mind. If our individual performance is perceived to be good and looks good, applause can be expected. That's the goal our culture pushes us toward. It's socialized into the very core of our being. But there's another influence at work pulling us in the same direction.

Yanking Our Own Chain

Having to do with *what we are* rather than the *influences surrounding us*, we all possess a strong, natural inclination or compulsion toward acquiring personal advantage. We're scripted from birth to manipulate, always on the lookout for clever ways to self-promote.

Social scientists have had a field day substantiating and illustrating this tendency that's woven into our basic fabric.

Anthropologists speak of *display behavior* to explain the universal compulsion to attract attention. For example, in many tribes prestigious women wear all their jewelry all the time so that others can calculate and be impressed by their wealth.

Social psychologists refer to *impression management*. Even an infant still in the crib who has no language skills knows how to turn on the charm to get the desired response from his or her mother. Teenagers often use the same ploy while flirting with members of the opposite sex.

Have you every noticed folks repeatedly circling the shopping mall parking lot to locate a spot only a few feet closer to the store? And we've all heard of wealthy people who risk everything to cheat people out of a few paltry bucks. Why? It seems we're prone to weigh the long- and short-term costs and benefits in every situation and make our choices based on sheer self-interest—what we consider to be beneficial to ourselves.

In the survey I distributed, one of the questions I posed was *Why are people hesitant/resistant to living their lives in anonymity?* Most of the respondents made reference to our compulsion to acquire praise and self-glorification. We crave it. And when we get it, we lap it up like thirsty animals.

Furthermore, there never seems to be a sufficient quantity to quell our need for more. It's as if we say, "Bring on plenty of acclaim and notoriety, and keep it flowing!" Here's a sampling of responses to my question:

"We're programmed to enjoy strokes" (Bob, computer analyst).

"It's so much more fabulous to soak in the glory. We're wired that way. Fame offers a pseudo form of love or adoration that temporarily makes us feel good" (Diane and Brad, editor and business executive).

"It comes from the human need to be recognized, loved, and needed. That's not possible if no one knows what you do and doesn't give you accolades for doing it" (Everett, editor).

"We find our value in what folks think about us, so we need to give them reason to think good of us. Most television is about getting recognized" (Dan, university president).

"To be anonymous is to counter the longing of sinful nature, which has now become the norm" (Kent, university professor).

"The cost of anonymous living is dear. We fear that good deeds will go unnoticed, that kindness will not have leverage, and that piety will be misunderstood to be a lack of ability or confidence" (Andrew, university president).

In a way, it's seems as if we live between two bookends. On one end are hurricane-like "cultural winds," which push us to crave recognition. On the opposite end is our natural "hard-drive," which pulls us away from living and giving anonymously. These two bookends team up to discourage us from living under the radar of recognition.

Combining forces, these two culprits constantly motivate us to seek applause. With this in mind, in desperation many of us ask how we can possibly avoid joining the colossal herd of egomaniacs.

Our first impulse might be to seek protection within the Christian community. After all, supposedly herein exist many who claim to be highly motivated to bring glory to God alone and resist the cultural push and inner pull to crave self-reward.

Within the Camp?

I doubt that you'll be shocked to learn that there are unfortunate instances of self-promotion among believers. Some are downright laughable. I recall a highly-esteemed leader who, when photographed in a group, cleverly insisted on always standing in the front row, left side. Then, when the picture was shown in a periodical, the caption below always listed his name first.

One of the survey respondents shared another story of self-promotion. She overheard a group discussing a church layman who was recognized as a mover and shaker. He was very wealthy, and to his credit, very generous. Unfortunately, he insisted on his name going on every building or program he supported. Once, when he was asked to lead in prayer, he prefaced his prayer with a reminder of his financial status and the phenomenal growth of his business. Although he's done much good, his reputation gets mixed reviews because of his counterproductive self-promotion.

Have you ever attended a slick, well-choreographed church musical presentation the sole purpose of which seemed to be to showcase personal talent rather than to draw worshipers' hearts and minds to the Almighty?

As within secular culture, push-and-pull factors within the church environment may dissuade us from embracing a low-key, quiet humility. A. W. Tozer once observed, "Christians have fallen into the habit of making the noisiest and most notorious among them as the best and the greatest."

Even ministers sometimes promote this spiritual distraction. Why? Most are held accountable by their denominations to report tangible results to determine the success of their ministries. Such results are external in nature—activities, programs, property, contributions—and become a part of statistical profiles that compare ministries to one another.

Because external goals must be accomplished, many clergy hold their noses and resort to stroking and doling out plaudits to bolster recognition for those who contribute—regardless of such persons' motivation.

I sympathize with leaders who find themselves in this position. They must struggle to find the balance between extending appreciation and inflating egos. They're pushed into a bona fide Catch 22.

Let's move to the pull factor within the church environment. Human nature again rears its ugly head to clamor for recognition. No doubt, some of this tendency is innocent and devoid of negative consequences.

However, an excessive hunger for acclaim often betrays a heart that's not cleansed by our Lord and not aligned with His purposes. It's vain—plain and simple.

By contrast, it's reassuring and refreshing to observe those who stubbornly resist both the relentless push and pull to self-promote. Instead, their sole intent is to offer their lives as living sacrifices, holy and acceptable unto God. (See Romans 12:1.) They don't seek parades or press conferences of public displays—they just do what's right with no desire for fanfare. They do what's right for Him alone.

Abraham Lincoln once said that to have one true friend is to be truly wealthy. In the same sense, to know one true-blue, under-the-radar-screen Christian is a treasure beyond measure. I'll share an incident from the life of one such Christian who had a profound effect on my life.

The Tardy Titan

Eugene Stowe was the respected and highly esteemed president of the seminary I attended—always standing tall and stately with a voice that resonated so deeply that he sounded as if he spoke from the bottom of a barrel. Dr. Stowe could hold his own with the best of scholars in theological discussions, pray with spiritual power, and preach with incredible impact without notes.

To those of us who know him, it was no surprise that he was eventually elected to the highest office in our denomination. As he effectively influenced policy and traveled about the world, hundreds of thousands were privileged to encounter this exceptional leader.

Dr. Stowe was scheduled to speak at a large rally in my brother's Texas church. People congregated from miles around, enthusiastically anticipating the event. The service began with a bang with awesome music. However, the speaker's chair was empty, and Dr. Stowe was nowhere in sight.

The prayer was offered. Announcements were made. The organizers of the event were getting nervous, and before long everyone seemed uneasy.

Just minutes before he was to be introduced, he came in through the side door, eliciting a collective deep sigh of relief. After being introduced, Dr. Stowe offered his sincere apology for being late. He said simply that he had been held up by an incident.

The sermon began and, as expected, it was another masterpiece, bringing God and congregation together. Those who heard it were deeply impacted.

No further reference was made to the speaker's tardiness. Everyone assumed that he must have had a good reason, because it wasn't his style to be late to anything. The next day, though, the cause of his late arrival was revealed. The church secretary answered a phone call, and on the line was a weak-voiced woman who said, "I've been trying all day to trace the whereabouts of an extremely kind gentleman. Last evening, my car conked out on a busy freeway. My children and I were stranded. It was beginning to get dark, and nobody had stopped to help us. Finally, a car pulled up. This very tall man got out, walked over to our car, and immediately put us at ease. He offered to take us to the nearest service station. He didn't just dump us off either, but he stayed with us until we were on our way. Then he left without leaving a card. He just wished us God's best and departed. I faintly recalled his name from when we first met and have spent the day tracking him down. I couldn't rest until I thanked him again for his extreme thoughtfulness. Will you please give him this message?"

The secretary fulfilled the request and joyfully shared the story. Those who heard it received a powerful *second* sermon from this godly man.

Dr. Stowe did not share the story with the congregation. He had no desire to play the crowd and call attention to himself. Yet his very life refreshes us and strengthens our resolve to bring glory to the Savior.

Discussion Questions:

1. Try to recall a time when you, like the frog, were just aching to declare to the world, "I did it!" What prompted you?

2. Have you encountered or heard about folks doing outlandish things to gain recognition? Please share.

3. What's your take on pumping up kids with a positive self-image—prior to actual achievement?

4. How do you feel pushed by cultural influences, or pulled by your own inner nature, to engage in self-promotion?

5. Do you believe Dr. Stowe had a justifiable reason for making the crowd wait? Why or why not?

Action Items

1. Get with friends and discuss "Good Samaritans" you've known. Discuss how you might become the same.

2. Write or call today someone who went out of his or her way to assist you. Include a token gift, small plaque, or gift certificate.

Section Two
Wise Biblical Admonition

Four
Bright Light Shining from the Shadows

Charles Swindoll declares that Jesus conquered two deadly temptations that constantly plague all of us. The first is *self-reliance* rather than God-dependence. The second is the *allure to be spectacular* rather than the allure to be inconspicuous. In doing so He had no resemblance to either Horatio Alger or Evil Knievel—if you catch my drift.

Paraphrasing John Henry Nouwen, our Lord refused to be a stunt man walking on hot coals, swallowing fire, or putting His hand into a lion's mouth in order to demonstrate His legitimacy. Unlike exhibitionists today, He refrained from grandstanding, polishing His image, or grasping for the limelight. Rather, He simply quietly and consistently went around doing good. (See Acts 10:38.)

Little Splash and Sparkle

Consider the circumstances of His birth. It took place in the quiet anonymity of an animal cave in an obscure village overshadowed by Jerusalem. The few who managed to find the location did so because of divine celestial assistance. No detailed map or GPS guided them.

No fireworks lit the sky, and no loud speakers drew attention to His birthplace. The only real celebration occurred within the overwhelmed hearts of His parents and reverent visitors.

Speaking of his parents, they were considered "people of the earth"—low in status and poor, without education or pedigree. We're clued in to their poverty by Mary's humble gift at the Temple on the customary eighth day following her Son's birth. Rather than a sheep, her offering was a pigeon—which typically only the lowly presented.

Furthermore, our Lord offered no pronouncements from His earthly crib, nor did He rise in magnificence to perform miracles with the flick of His tiny, infant hand. He lay there on the cattle straw, bundled up and with a sweet smile.

That first Christmas quickly vanished. The great star in the East faded. The glorious melodies of the choir of angels melted into the Judean hills. The few who had come to behold Him worshiped, left their gifts, and began the long trek homeward. Jesus was left with His mother and foster father to grow up in Nazareth, a place considered even more underwhelming than tiny Bethlehem.

For whatever reasons, the years of his youth and young adulthood weren't recorded. I surmise that as He matured in all ways (see Luke 2:52), His life consisted of normal activities. As the oldest, His carpenter craftsman skills no doubt provided support for His mother and siblings. This was especially crucial due to, according to most biblical scholars, Joseph's premature death.

Like other Jewish males of His day, Jesus' days were routine, perhaps even humdrum, though certainly not insignificant. He probably labored in the shop, assisted His mother with household tasks, spent time in the synagogue schooling himself in the Law, and took walks into the nearby hills or to Sephoris, the grandiose, Greek-style city three miles away that offered cosmopolitan opportunities.

Is it too difficult for us to imagine our Lord, for most of His brief stay on earth, doing ordinary stuff in the shadows of obscurity? Evidently it was impossible for Gnostic authors. Leaping far beyond honest documentary, these presented Jesus in a fanciful, fictitious manner. One of their yarns portrayed Him molding clay pigeons, then flinging them upward into the heavens to fly—as crowds went bananas in exaltation!

Such bizarre tales fail to square with the tenor of His life and ministry. In short, they are drastically out of line with the character of Jesus. Jesus himself rejected such temptations from the "father of lies" as when He was urged to jump from the Temple's pinnacle. Thankfully, the Church judged the Gnostic pseudo-accounts for what they were: sharp contradiction to His divine nature.

We can know with certainty that our Savior, who performed many—possibly most—of His greatest miracles secretly and commanded that they remain unheralded, would never make such a mockery of truth.

His low-profile approach is also apparent in His preferred form of teaching. He used parables—common language metaphors about everyday occurrences—none of which accentuated the magical or ostentatious. Most were presented in simple settings: in fishing boats, grain fields, and on green hillsides.

He could have been a showboat, had He so chosen, like none before or since, for His potential was unbounded. Recall how as a lad of 12 He astounded the Temple scholars with His vast wisdom and ability to communicate. But while always speaking with authority and pathos, He also spoke without pretense. He chose to reject the spectacular in favor of plain speech, knowing that it best complemented His calling, purpose, and mission.

Relinquishing Vast Options

Many of us dream of going out in style. Major leaguers yearn to hit a round-tripper their final time at bat or, even better, to pitch a no-hitter. Ministers envision entering the pulpit for the last time to deliver their greatest, most impacting and anointed sermon ever. Even suicide bombers hope to make that final blast one that will result in the death of scores of their enemies.

Multitudes from all walks of life make it a high priority to assure that their final act is their best. To do so, they reason, is to greatly enhance their chances of being remembered with great esteem—by people or by God.

Was Jesus motivated by this desire? Far from it. He recoiled from earthly fame and chose an ignominious final act—not dazzling, not honorific. Rather, just the opposite: one of extreme disgrace. As a matter of fact, many judged Him a dismal failure—a person whose message was rendered inauthentic by His demise—much to the glee of His enemies.

Except to His followers, His death was perceived as that of a common criminal. And He willingly accepted that verdict, refusing to change that perception with any awesome display of power.

He could have escaped His predicament in an eye blink; His options were limitless. Angels were doubtlessly poised to pounce. All beings and forces of nature stood at the ready.

But our love-driven Lord chose to renounce any sensational trump cards that would have freed Him from this inconceivable ordeal. Instead, He went as a sheep to the slaughter, opting to even keep His escape options His secret! (See Acts 8:32.)

On the first Easter morning the glorious Resurrection occurred, once and for all establishing that His battle had been won. It seems that if ever He had justification to revel and rejoice, it would be at that time. Amazingly, though, even this—the greatest cosmic event of all time—was accomplished in secret.

Roman guards who could have witnessed it had fallen asleep. Even after the event occurred, Jesus refused to reveal himself to Mary Magdalene in the Garden, although she recognized Him. On the road to Emmaus He omitted telling the disciples His name. As Mary had, they put two and two together as they observed His signature humility while breaking bread.

He didn't burst into the Upper Room heralded by trumpets. Instead, He unobtrusively slipped into their midst. And after sighting His disciples on the Sea of Galilee, He didn't yell out, "Hey, look at me—I'm your risen Lord!" Instead, He calmly called out, "Children, have you any fish?" (See *The Secret and Humble God, A Holy Week Reflection,* by Antony Hughes.)

Downplaying things as He did, is it any wonder that our sovereign Lord's earthly sojourn is almost exclusively ignored by secular historians of His day? Is it a stretch for us to assume that He preferred it that way? Let's explore a couple of important reasons.

Behind His Intentions

Jesus knew that He must somehow dissuade people from seeing Him as a rip-roaring political or military savior. He well knew how desperate they were to free themselves from Rome's oppression. He also realized that accounts of His miracles had roared through the country like a brush fire, causing people's hope to soar as they anticipated that He might be the one to liberate them from Rome's domination.

Furthermore, our Lord fully anticipated the depths of their disappointment and anger when they realized that His kingdom was not of this world and that His means of ascendancy had nothing to do with force or pomp and circumstance or settling a score with a powerful, oppressive world empire.

Attempting to tamp down their wild anticipation, He chose to be as inconspicuous as possible in order to buy time. Otherwise, His hallowed plans and purposes couldn't be fully realized. If forced to rush, He was aware that His divine goals could be seriously thwarted.

Our Lord was here on a very special assignment, and only He clearly understood its scope, details, and purposes. His was an assignment that required sufficient time, dictating that He must live and minister, for the most part, anonymously and off center stage.

He also firmly believed that a life of anonymity was the most consistent with what He valued most—humility, meekness, servanthood. Not the slightest disconnect existed between our Savior's admonitions concerning these great qualities of heart and how He consistently lived. The person of Jesus and the proclamation were identically aligned.

I'm amazed by today's higher echelon of terrorist leaders who strongly urge their followers to strap on explosives and sacrifice themselves for what they tout as a noble and holy cause. Meanwhile, these cowardly spokespersons recoil at the very thought of following their own advice.

Contrast that with our Lord's actions on the somber evening before His betrayal and death. In that Upper Room, He quietly and inconspicuously washed His disciples' feet. It was the ritual of a bona fide servant. It was in perfect synchrony with what He had asked of His followers. He was an unmistakable do-as-I-do Savior rather than a hypocritical do-as-I-say leader.

He made His point and underscored it by simply walking His talk. He consistently and anonymously embodied His life-giving message. In doing so, He gives His words unquestionable authority and reliability.

Having focused on the life of Jesus, let's direct our attention to His actual words. What did He declare about the life of anonymity? Granted, such a life was essential for Him, but might it be optional for His followers? To what areas does it especially pertain? What primacy did He give to this vital issue?

We're assured of the exalted importance Jesus ascribed to anonymity by virtue of its inclusion in His Sermon on the Mount. Let's examine a few significant facts concerning the greatest sermon ever preached.

Epic Words, Great Wisdom

Through the ages, scholars have termed this sermon such things as "the compendium of Christ's doctrine," "the Magna Carta of the Kingdom," and "the manifesto of the King." But the one that seems to me to be closest to its primary intent is "the ordination address to the Twelve." Luke's account of it is followed immediately by the choosing of the Twelve.

The core and distillation of our Lord's teaching was presented to His chosen inner circle so they would propagate it accurately. Furthermore, according to commentator William Barclay, it's likely that that the Sermon on the Mount wasn't delivered in one day.

In *The Christ of the Mount: A Working Philosophy of Life,* E. Stanley Jones declares that this spiritual masterpiece is none other than an awesome verbal portrait of Jesus himself.

> As He draws the lines in the picture . . . He dips His brush into the deeps of His own life and experience, and gradually [there appears] that "one dear Face." . . . We have here not the lines of a code but the lineaments of His character (27).

Is it revolutionary in tone? Absolutely, for it cuts squarely across the grain of the typical self-centered life.

The Sermon on the Mount is light-years beyond being just another sermon or document. It inculcates the essence of our Lord's teaching and as such provides the quintessential moral compass for us all. It is not something to consider lightly or treat with a cavalier take-it-or-leave-it attitude.

It was while I was meditating upon this inspiring sermon that the importance of anonymous living hit me. Let's examine this beloved and blessed sermon with open minds and receptive hearts.

Three Great Pillars of the Good Life

> Be especially careful when you are trying to be good so that you don't make a performance out of it. It might be good theater, but the God who made you won't be applauding.
>
> When you do something for someone else, don't call attention to yourself. You've seen them in action, I'm sure—"playactors" I call them—treating prayer meeting and street corner alike as a stage, acting compassionate as long as someone is watching, playing to the crowds. They get applause, true, but that's all they get. When you help someone out, don't think about how it looks. Just do it—quietly and unobtrusively. That is the way your God, who conceived you in love, working behind the scenes, helps you out.

And when you come before God, don't turn that into a theatrical production either. All these people making a regular show out of their prayers, hoping for stardom! Do you think God sits in a box seat?

Here's what I want you to do: Find a quiet, secluded place so you won't be tempted to role-play before God. Just be there as simply and honestly as you can manage. The focus will shift from you to God, and you will begin to sense his grace.

The world is full of so-called prayer warriors who are prayer-ignorant. They're full of formulas and programs and advice, peddling techniques for getting what you want from God. Don't fall for that nonsense. This is your Father you are dealing with, and he knows better than you what you need. With a God like this loving you, you can pray very simply....

When you practice some appetite-denying discipline to better concentrate on God, don't make a production out of it. It might turn you into a small-time celebrity but it won't make you a saint. If you "go into training" inwardly, act normal outwardly. Shampoo and comb your hair, brush your teeth, wash your face. God doesn't require attention-getting devices. He won't overlook what you are doing; he'll reward you well *(Matthew 6:1-8; 16-18, TM)*.

For Jews in Christ's day, there were three great pillars upon which the good life was built: almsgiving, prayer, and fasting. Jesus had no bone to pick with any of these spiritual disciplines, but He was greatly troubled by folks who did them for personal glory.

Someone who contributes big bucks may do so not to express compassion but to parade generosity and bask in the warmth of others' praise. Likewise, a man may pray like a bishop but rather than sincerely addressing God intend only to parade his piety. Finally, a woman may fast until she's anorexic, not to humble herself before God but to impress others with her self-discipline.

Let's examine these three venerated activities and view them from two contrasting periods: Christ's day and our own.

Almsgiving

For almsgiving, considered the most sacred of all religious duties, the Jews used the same word, *tzedakah,* for "righteousness." Giving alms and being righteous were considered one and the same, and as such, it atoned for sins.

It might be surprising to realize that rabbinical teaching advocated that money be given in secret. One rabbi often dropped money behind him so that he wouldn't see who picked it up. With the same intent, a special room, "the chamber of the silent," existed in the Temple, where persons left money to atone for their sins. From such funds the poor were secretly assisted.

The ideal of secret giving was often not attained, though. During services, when offerings were taken for the poor, givers-turned-grandstanders made certain that others knew how much they gave.

Whether back then or today, three motives underlie giving. First is the grim and self-righteous compulsion of *duty*—from which there is no perceived escape. Some even see the poor as existing to enable this duty to be fulfilled.

Second, some give to attain *prestige*—to climb in status. If such a person isn't aptly rewarded, he or she is usually very discontent, because his or her monetary investment failed to result in elevated, enhanced honor.

Third, others *give as Christ gave*—from an upsurge of love, kindliness, or a sense of responsibility that gushes forth from the giver's heart, spilling out to those in need. This is the cheerful giving mentioned in 2 Corinthians 9:7 that pleases God most. It's clear that Jesus gave in such a joyful, spontaneous manner. "Though he was rich, yet for your sakes he became poor, so that you through his poverty might become rich" (2 Corinthians 8:9).

Those who give this way are the most likely to give anonymously. They have no axes to grind, people to impress, or obligations to perform. They give in openhanded, openhearted response compelled by a deep, inner compulsion to do good—and to do so without any demand of public recognition.

Prayer

No nation ever had a higher ideal of prayer than Israel, nor has any religion ever ranked it higher on the scale of priorities than Judaism. This goes for public prayer as well as that which occurs within the home. It has been said that he who prays within his house surrounds it with a wall that's stronger than iron.

As with almsgiving, certain glaring faults crept into the customary prayer of Christ's day—not faults of neglect, so typical today, but rather grievous errors of misguided devotion. And of these, Jesus considered praying to be seen by others to be the most damaging.

The Jewish system of prayer made ostentation very easy. Meet Jehuda, a faithful Pharisee. His very prayer posture sets him apart; he stands praying with hands outstretched, palms upward, and head bowed. He "freezes" to pray at 9:00 A.M., 12 midday, and 3 P.M. each day, regardless of where he is. He conveniently arranges to position himself at these hours in very conspicuous locations: a busy street corner, a crowded city square, the top entrance step of the synagogue. In such places Jehuda prays lengthily and demonstratively for scores to observe.

It is only fair to mention that the wisest Jewish rabbis would soundly condemn Jehuda's "traveling-road-show" attitude. (See Matthew 7:6, TM.) To them, his theatrics smacked of hypocrisy. Their verdict was that the prayers of such a man are not heard. In their minds a perfect prayer required an hour of private preparation beforehand and an hour of meditation afterward. Nevertheless, the point remains: the Jewish system of prayer undeniably left itself open to ostentation and arrogance.

In His sermon Jesus was in effect telling Jehuda and others like him that there are two quintessential, absolutely reliable rules regarding authentic prayer.

All true prayer must be offered to God. Jehuda's primary concern was praying to impress others. Simply put, it was a performance, a show geared to wow the audience.

In recent times I've heard public prayers that seemed more targeted to impressing the congregation than connecting with our Heavenly Father. This could be why scholarly, erudite, written prayers—in contrast to spontaneous, conversational ones—seem less impacting. Though appropriate at times, they may have a marked tendency to showcase the one praying at the expense of exonerating God.

This in no way implies that public prayers should totally disregard the congregation and their needs or situational challenges. But the point remains—our primary focus must be galvanized on Him to whom we pray.

We must always remember that our God of love is far more ready and eager to answer than we are to pray. We don't have to wrench His gifts and grace from Him. He need not be coaxed, pestered, or battered into answering our prayers, though we're encouraged to be courteously and confidently persistent. (See the parable of the persistent widow in Luke 18:1-8.)

Contrast the frenzied prayer of 450 Baal prophets on Mount Carmel with that of Elijah. The former went through all sorts of contortions, including slashing themselves and shouting—from morning to noon—to get their god's attention.

Enter cool, collected, confident Elijah, who employed only 58 words —which barely consumed a mere 20 seconds allowing for pauses. The ending of his brief prayer makes a simple, straightforward request for the benefit of his people:

> Answer me, LORD, answer me, so these people will know that you, LORD, are God, and that you are turning their hearts back again *(1 Kings. 18:36-37).*

The result was undeniable. All those at the scene were convinced that Elijah served the one true God. It wasn't necessary for Him to be awakened, aroused, or annoyed by long verbiage or extreme physical gyrations. As Jesus said, He was, and is always, poised and ready to lovingly respond.

Indeed, our blessed Abba's deep desire is to give to His children. (See Matthew 7:9-11; Luke 11:11-13.) When we remember this, we approach Him with supremely confident hearts and with lips that are quick to utter those hallowed words "Thy will be done."

The Sermon on the Mount declares that our words to Him are best spoken in secret (see Matthew 6:6) from our closets, while walking alone on the beach, or on a lonely hospital bed. Admittedly, this doesn't approximate the spectacular in this world's eyes, but it's infinitely precious to Him and ultimately invaluable to us!

Fasting

For Jews, during our Lord's sojourn on earth, only the Day of Atonement was a compulsory fast day. On that day, from morning until evening, all men had to "afflict their souls" (Leviticus 16:31, KJV). According to scribal law, it was forbidden to eat, drink, bathe, anoint oneself, wear sandals, or indulge in sex. In addition to this special national day, Jews also engaged in private fasting.

There are at least four important reasons fasting was practiced: First, it was a blatant attempt to attract God's attention. God was perceived as being very preoccupied. Second, it was no doubt intended to make it seem that penitent words were sincere and straight from the heart. Third, it was an activity intended to counterbalance deficiencies of piety, an attempt to atone for not having a sterling track record, much like purchasing an extravagant birthday gift to make up for a year of negligence. Finally, there was the showboating feature, whereby the typical fasting countenance was used to impress others.

Although the first three were sorely deficient, the fourth was especially abhorrent to Jesus. At its core, the showboating factor tied itself in with the rank exhibitionism also evident in almsgiving and prayer.

The Jewish days of fasting, Monday and Thursday, happened to be market days when multitudes poured into Jerusalem from the countryside. Thus, those who created a spectacle of their fasting could play to a large audience at the market.

Jehuda and others went overboard in taking deliberate measures to ensure that no one would miss the fact that they were fasting. They paraded through the streets with their hair unkempt and disheveled, their clothes were deliberately soiled and disarrayed, and their faces were whitened to accentuate their paleness.

The wisest of rabbis condemned this as unsparingly as Jesus did. They were convinced that fasting for its own sake had no value. As they put it, it was much like sticking one's head into a collar and finding that he or she had voluntarily undertaken a useless slavery. One rabbi declared that a person must give an account on Judgment Day for every good thing he or she might have enjoyed and refused to.

A crucial point related to fasting is that although Jesus condemned the wrong kind of fasting, He didn't throw out the baby with the bath water. Unfortunately, most of us ignore the value of fasting and don't practice it today. Jesus demonstrated and described a fasting that's wise and holy and done without fanfare, seeking only the mastery of our bodies for God's glory.

That implies refraining from donning fasting costumes or long and somber faces. Instead, it means remaining consistently normal and appearing to be inconspicuously natural.

(For further study, see William Barclay's *Daily Study Bible* [Philadelphia: Westminster Press, 1958].)

Example+Wise Words=Impact

Jesus walked His talk, and He talked His walk. Both His walk and talk portrayed the one who projected a great spotlight of truth—but mostly from the shadows. That was not without good reason.

To follow in the footsteps of Jesus and to obey His teaching is to live and give inconspicuously. We're not to imagine ourselves onstage, engaging in a theatrical production in order to hear thunderous applause. The only one whose approval we most need does not occupy a box seat. And even if He did, He wouldn't be the least bit impressed by our performance—even if it were to contain great quantities of generosity, piety, or self-discipline.

Discussion Questions:

1. Why do religious Christmas pageants reveal such a fictitious picture of our Lord's birth, especially downplaying its lack of glitz and glamour?

2. How difficult is it to wrap your mind around Jesus contenting himself with ordinary, low-profile activities between the ages of 12 and 30, His so-called silent years? Why is it so difficult for us to see the significance of the routine?

3. Rather than seeking fame, our Lord took measures to intentionally downplay His notoriety. What measures did He take? Have you known anyone who was sought after but who attempted to get people to back off?

4. Related to living anonymously, what word, idea, or phrase in the paraphrase of the Sermon on the Mount found in *The Message* impacted or inspired you the most? Explain.

5. Of the three venerated activities—almsgiving, prayer, and fasting—which one is the greatest temptation for Christians, or you, to parade? Explain. Why is fasting put on the back burner for most of us? Should the practice be resurrected?

Action Items

1. Start a secret fund among your friends to anonymously dispense money to those in need. Establish your own rules, and join in praying for recipients.

2. Take a gradual approach to fasting—at first fasting only periodically for specific reasons. Then adopt it as a life-habit. And above all, do so inconspicuously and anonymously.

Five
God's Ordinary People

God often uses ordinary people—folks unimpressed with themselves and unimpressive to others—to fulfill His greatest tasks. Also, He gets great delight in baffling the wise.

Being ordinary, however, is far from a cherished goal in our world today. In his book *Whatever Happened to Ordinary Christians,* Jim Smoke underscores this truth: "In the age of the sensational, the superb, and the extraordinary, who in his right mind wants to be ordinary? Ordinary is vanilla when everyone wants pistachio; plain wrap when everyone wants fancy; average when everyone wants exceptional; being back in the line when everyone wants to be first; not attracting attention when everyone wants it." Smoke's conclusion is that "Ordinary is simply not in."

But, to quote Abraham Lincoln, "God must love ordinary people, because He made so many of them." He loves the generic, the commonplace, the run-of-the-mill, not just those who are off the charts in ability, wealth, intelligence, personality, or appearance. But even though God might consider ordinary people special, few others do.

That's why most ordinary folks live simply and outside the glow of the limelight. You might wonder why such persons are the ones our Lord typically chooses to use in a big way. I believe it could be because they seem far more likely to fully depend on Him and to be the clay in the potter's hands.

This is likely why the apostle Paul placed a premium on ordinary Christians. He explains that the Corinthians were confused and carnal because they kept running around looking for extraordinary signs, wonders, and experiences. Pulling them back to reality, he lays it on the line:

> Brothers, think of what you were when you were called. Not many of you were wise by human standards; not many were influential; not many were of noble birth. But God chose the foolish things of the world to shame the wise; God chose the weak things of the world to shame the strong . . . so that no one can boast before him" (1 Corinthians 1:26-27, 29).

Indeed, God has a penchant for choosing ordinary folks. After being so chosen and fulfilling His assignment, many ordinaries return to being inconspicuous. Recall the lad who supplied loaves and fish to feed the multitude. After relinquishing his sack lunch and witnessing the miracle, he melted into anonymity.

On the other hand, other ordinary persons tapped on the shoulder by God engage in a lifetime of very significant, highly visible service. Consider Moses, reluctant leader of the estimated three million Israelites who fled Pharaoh's wrath. He had both a speech impediment and a "rap sheet" revealing his murder of an Egyptian. Exemplary? Not on paper. But God saw his true, underlying potential.

In spite of this world's faulty assessment, ordinary people who respond to God's voice should not be labeled as insignificant—especially if they remain humble. Why? Because they've discovered the pathway to true greatness—an unwavering dependence on the true source of all strength.

They've realized that God desires their accessibility more than their abilities.

Whoops! You Have the Wrong Person

I love first reactions. When people are caught by surprise, their responses are often very humorous, especially when asked to tackle something far beyond their perceived ability, especially when the someone doing the asking is their Heavenly Father.

Consider these initial responses of persons who went on to make the A list of biblical personalities. All have the same initial response: *God, I lack the credentials, pedigree, and ability. With all due respect, you're making a serious mistake. Others are far more qualified.*

Gideon: "My clan is the weakest in Manasseh, and I am the least in my family" (Judges 6:15).

Saul: "But am I not a Benjamite, from the smallest tribe of Israel, and is not my clan the least of all the clans of the tribe of Benjamin?" (1 Samuel 9:21).

David: "Who am I, and what is my family or my father's clan in Israel?" (1 Samuel 18:18). "I'm only a poor man and little known" (v. 23). "Whom are you pursuing? A dead dog? A flea?" (1 Samuel 24:14).

Solomon: "But I am only a little child and do not know how to carry out my duties" (1 Kings 3:7).

Amos: "I was neither a prophet nor a prophet's son, but I was a shepherd, and I also took care of sycamore-fig trees" (Amos 7:14).

Prior to their calling, most of the above lived faithful, anonymous lives. But as a field that lies fallow enables the soil to become enriched for future planting, these stalwarts remained low-profile until God's time arrived. Thereafter, their rule and their ministries were epically significant.

Now let's examine a few biblical personalities who lived their entire lives faithfully doing good, often at great cost, without playing to the crowd. In fact, seeking adulation was at the bottom of their wish list. Their anonymity-with-contentment should inspire us all to choose this wise course.

SECTION 2

Old Testament Low-profilers

Naomi

Naomi's home was Bethlehem in the dark days of the Judges, when "everyone did as he saw fit." (See Judges 17:6; 21:25.) A famine occurred, prompting her husband, Elimelech, two sons, Mahlon and Kilion, and Naomi to move to Moab, east of the Dead Sea.

Bad blood existed between the two nations. Moab had disallowed the Jews to pass through their land during the Exodus. Since that time, relations with its people were severely strained and strongly discouraged. (See Deuteronomy 23:3-6.) Moabites were prohibited even from worshiping in the Jewish tabernacle.

A short time after arriving, Naomi's husband passed away. Ten years later, her sons, who had married Moabite women, also died. That left Naomi and her daughters-in-law, Ruth and Orpah, alone.

Being widows in the ancient world implied being taken advantage of, ignored, and impoverished. Granted, God's law assigned the closest relative of the dead husband to care for the widow, but none of the three had relatives in Moab, nor were they aware of any kin alive in Israel. They were destitute.

Then welcome news arrived that the famine was over, and the three desperate women set out for Israel. It was then that Naomi halted the procession and selflessly advised them to return to Moab and remarry. She fully realized that if they took her advice, she would be abandoned and completely alone in an inhospitable world.

Although both daughters-in-law wept and offered to continue on, Orpah was finally convinced to turn back. Naomi pled with Ruth to join her sister. It was then that Ruth uttered these touching, immortal words that have often since been repeated by brides to their grooms:

> Where you go I will go, and where you stay I will stay. Your people will be my people and your God my God (*Ruth 1:16*).

Naomi and Ruth returned to Bethlehem. In God's trustworthy

providence, they were led to Boaz, a kinsman-redeemer who provided them with sustenance and eventually married Ruth. Then God overdid it a little—which is not unlike Him. Their son Obed was born and eventually became grandfather to no less than King David!

Why is Naomi a sterling example of an anonymous servant of God? The reasons are very apparent. First, she embraced persons who were hated by her native country, making her an incredible model of genuine, spiritual character and forgiveness, a model that God's chosen nation had heretofore failed to exhibit.

Second, her quiet, consistent, godly character grew on her daughters-in-law, especially Ruth, until they yearned to remain with her, embracing her people and her faith.

Third, as alluded to, she showed selflessness in urging both to return to their own people—this while facing the dire consequences of her aloneness. One could convincingly argue that she demonstrated servanthood at a time when she faced incredible uncertainty and risk.

Although on what must have been a very bad day she blamed God and said the "Almighty has made my life very bitter" (Ruth 1:20), she never ceased to trust Him. She eventually clearly saw how He had produced blessing out of tragedy. This blessing consisted of a loving soul mate, a return home, a path-crossing with Boaz, and for toppers, a destiny-enriched grandson whom she lovingly "laid on her lap and cared for" (Ruth 4:16).

Naomi. Loyal and faithful wife and mother. Loving in accepting a new land and alien daughters-in-law. Courageous in being willing to relinquish her security. Helpful in giving guidance to Ruth as she reestablished herself. And all done inconspicuously and without fanfare. Naomi, we pray to possess your spunk and humility!

Eli

Eli was the revered priest at Shiloh and esteemed judge of all Israel. Nevertheless, his own house was in sad and chaotic disarray. His two sons, Hophni and Phinehas, meaning "Tadpole" and "Nubian," although receiving nepotistic appointments to the priesthood, gave anguishing grief to their father.

The two reprobates "had no regard for the Lord" (1 Samuel 2:12), treated with contempt "the offering of the Lord" (v. 17) as well as "all the Israelites who came" to Shiloh (v. 14), and "lay with the women who served at the entrance to the tent of meeting" (v. 22). Eli scolded them for their wicked behavior, but his attempts at tough love seemed only to make them worse. They stubbornly refused to shape up (vv. 22-25).

While these heartbreaking events occurred, something very positive began to unfold. It began when a devout mother, Hannah, made a pilgrimage to Shiloh and quietly prayed for God to give her a son—vowing to dedicate him to His holy service. Eli, perhaps a tad senile, overheard and mistook her prayer for the inaudible mutterings of an inebriated woman. But shortly after rebuking her, he realized his error and bent over backwards to make amends. It gives a kind of comfort to realize that even a God-appointed high priest isn't immune from making a bonehead mistake.

True to her word, soon after baby Samuel was weaned, Hannah brought him to Shiloh. There he began his lifelong service as a Nazirite under Eli. (See 1 Samuel 1:24-28; 2:11.) After entering childhood, God gave the promising lad a very personal call—which Eli patiently helped him to fully own and understand.

Thereafter, Samuel "ministered before the Lord" (1 Samuel 2:11, 18; 3:1), "grew up in the presence of the Lord" (2:21), and "continued to grow both in stature and in favor with the LORD and with men" (2:26). All thanks to Eli—his wise and holy mentor.

Meanwhile, an unnamed prophet approached Eli to drop a verbal bomb. Eli was told that the grievous sins of his sons would result in God's harsh judgment and that his priestly line would be cut off and superseded by that of another (vv. 27-36).

The same dire message was repeated and reinforced by Samuel himself—who now served as the conduit of God's word to the now aged priest. Furthermore, Eli was informed that the day of reckoning was coming, in part because *he* had failed to restrain his sons' evil conduct. To his credit, Eli accepted the inevitable as a sign of the Lord's displeasure and rebuke (1 Samuel 3:11-18).

After a severe military defeat suffered by the Israelites at the hands of the Philistines, Hophni and Phinehas accompanied the ark of the covenant onto the battlefield. (See 1 Samuel 4:1-4.) The elders had ordered the ark to be brought out of the Tabernacle and into battle as a talisman to assure Israel's victory. Although fearful, the Philistines fought bravely and captured the ark. Apparently Eli's two sons were among the casualties who died in the battle (vv. 10-11).

By this time Eli was an obese old man, 98 years of age and nearly blind. When he heard the report of the death of his sons and the capture of the ark, the shock was such that he fell backward off his chair, broke his neck, and died.

He had been a judge in Israel for 40 years. Longevity should count for a lot. Undeniably, he was a tragic figure—helplessly unable to corral his sons. Indeed, the prophecy concerning the demise of his line was eventually fulfilled, reverting to the bloodline of Eleazar.

Rather that throwing up his hands in desperation and total surrender, this man of God redirected his efforts to young Samuel. The result was that Samuel soaked up all that Eli offered and thereby thoroughly prepared himself for an incredibly significant life of godly service.

What a great lesson for many of us today! While doing our best as parents, we must not cease doing good if our children choose to defy our instruction and reject our love. Like Eli, we must extend a helping hand and compassionate heart to others beyond our immediate family. We should do this consistently, selflessly, and without a desire for notoriety or acclaim.

Naomi and Eli were exemplary, beneath-the-radar servants. Let's examine a couple of servants who lived during New Testament times.

SECTION 2

New Testament Spotlight-Avoiders

Andrew

In an earlier chapter we talked about bridge people—persons who reach out to span gaps in order to connect persons with those who are able to provide them with needed assistance. Such individuals aren't typically on an ego trip, for they must admit to themselves and others that they are unable to dispense the required help. Once again, these bridgers have but one rather unspectacular function: to be a mere conduit, to link those who *can* help with those who *need* help.

Nobody in the New Testament, save Jesus himself, is more deserving of the bridge person designation than the disciple Andrew. As such, he has always been a very special inspiration to me. We possess very little information about him, but what we do know reveals two extremely commendable traits.

First, Andrew was more than satisfied to take second place. Repeatedly he's tagged with one identifying designation—*Simon Peter's brother*. Unlike his famous sibling, Andrew wasn't one of the inner circle of disciples. When Jesus healed Jairus's daughter, went up to the Mount of Transfiguration, and underwent His temptation in Gethsemane, it was Peter, James, and John He took with Him.

It would have been so easy for Andrew to cop an attitude. After all, was he not one of the first two disciples to follow Jesus? Did Peter not owe his meeting with Jesus to Andrew? With these facts in mind, was it not only fair that he should be granted a high-profile position in the apostolic band?

But none of that dawned on Andrew. He was content to stand back in the shadows and let his more famous brother be in the limelight—to play second fiddle in the company of the Twelve. To him, matters of precedence, place, and honor counted for nothing. All that truly mattered was to be with Jesus and serve Him as he could. As such, according to William Barclay in *The Daily Study Bible: The Gospel of John, Vol. 1*, "Andrew is the patron saint of all who humbly and loyally and ungrudgingly take the second place." No doubt, that was a huge reason for his being such an exemplary bridger.

The second admirable trait exhibited by Andrew was that he found his greatest joy in introducing others to Jesus. Only three times did he enter center stage. The first was when he brought Peter to Jesus. After hearing John speak about Jesus, he rushed to find Simon at the crack of dawn the next morning. He boldly announced to Simon, "We have found the Messiah" (John 1:41). He then brought Simon to Jesus—who told him that thereafter he would be called *Cephas* (Peter), meaning "a rock" (v. 42).

A second incident was when Andrew brought the boy with the five loaves and two small fishes to Jesus. (See John 6:8-9.) He saw a need, possibly envisioned a miracle, negotiated with the boy, and led him, along with his humble food fragments, to the Lord. And the whole world knows what happened next.

The final incident occurred when Andrew brought inquiring Greeks, who had come to the Feast of the Passover, into the presence of Jesus. They approached Philip saying, "Sir, we want to see Jesus. Can you help us?" (John 12:20-21, TM). Philip went and told Andrew, and the two together told Jesus. The result was that the Greeks received eternal truth.

Andrew's greatest joy was to bridge others to Jesus, the one who had all the answers and could meet every need. He did it without making a big splash; he made no loud announcements. Rather, he chose to be an anonymous bridge person. Having found the friendship of Jesus, he spent the rest of his life inconspicuously introducing others to that friendship. He could not keep the secret to himself; he was determined to share, without hoopla or fanfare.

Mary, Mother of Jesus

For centuries uncivil Protestant vs. Catholic wrangling has obliterated any chance for meaningful dialog. The result is that what was embraced by one side received harsh, knee-jerk rejections from those with an opposing view. Favorite targets of Protestants have been saints, statuary, and recited prayers such as the Rosary. But the main target has been the Catholic portrayal of Mary.

Instead of asking who the real Mary was, there have been raging debates over what she was *not*: sinless, immaculately conceived, nonsexual, and so on. Sadly, such Mary debates have caused Protestants to remain detached and distant. As Scot McKnight sums it up in "The Mary We Never Knew" published in *Christianity Today,* "Consequently, [Mary became] a delicate piece in a Christmas crèche, who is brought out without comment at Christmas ... then wrapped up gently until next Advent."

Signs suggest that Protestants are finally becoming eager to give Mary her due. For example, recent books such as Tim Perry's *Mary for Evangelicals* have greatly elevated the discussion. It is dawning on non-Catholic Christians that Mary belongs to them too! And indications are that Catholics seem to concur.

Mary is the prototype of the anonymous saint. Never seeking attention, Mary "treasured up all these things and pondered them in her heart" (Luke 2:19).

Mary lived in the shadows, a widow striving to make ends meet, increasingly distanced from her Son, whose future she anguished over—and without any trace of bitterness.

Gibraltars of the Faith

The "Gibraltars of the faith" were four ordinary persons called upon to complete assignments much too big for them to accomplish on their own. They depended on God; they had no choice. They were overwhelmed. They never took bows. They knew very well that all the credit belonged to their God, who appointed and empowered them.

They were stalwart, steady, and content to live mostly in secret. Although their accomplishments had eternal implications, they possessed an aversion for hoopla, grandstanding, and spotlights. They desired to be grateful, faithful, obedient, and to give all glory to the God they intensely loved.

Discussion Questions:

1. If God's biblical heroes of choice seem to be ordinary folks, why are we so enamored by those who are in the limelight? On the other hand, cite instances of persons with extraordinary gifts being used by God. What is the lesson?

2. Do you know of instances of people attempting to beg off after God asked them to do something because they felt unqualified or unprepared? What's the most prevalent reason for doing so? Do you think it's humility, low self-esteem, or laziness?

3. Was Naomi justified when she blamed God for her misfortune? Are we? If so, under what circumstances and conditions? Did Eli sufficiently atone for blowing it with his two natural sons by the exemplary parenting job he did with Samuel?

4. What is your take on Andrew, who did plenty of sneaking around and doing good? Do you know anyone like that? If *you've* ever been a "holy sneak," what was the result?

5. In your opinion, what is Mary's "rightful place?" Do you feel that she has been ignored or misjudged for too long? On a personal note, in what specific way does she most inspire you in your Christian walk?

Action Items:

1. Select one of the biblical personalities discussed: Naomi, Eli, Andrew, or Mary. Go to a quiet place, say a prayer and ask God to open your mind and heart, and slowly read the account of that person's life. As you read, have a pad to jot down random, free-flowing thoughts about the person and applications to your own life. If you found this valuable, do the same with one or more of the remaining three.

2. Boaz purposely and compassionately left stalks of grain in his fields for the needy. Go to a restaurant and provide the owner or cashier with enough money to pay the next customer's bill—needy or not. Write words similar to these on a small piece of paper: "This is given with gratitude for God's goodness to me and with a prayer for your life. Have a great day."

3. As Andrew did, *link* someone with a source of help. You might purchase a book or share a CD that seems especially relevant to a person's situation. Or you might be the intermediary in bridging two persons—especially another with our Lord.

Six
Two Strategies, One Goal

Jungle. Shark tank. Boxing ring. War zone. Take your pick. All four are fitting metaphors for academia's ruthless, eat-or-be-eaten environment. To survive or gain traction, unfortunately, some succumb to unethical tactics. They plagiarize others' work, concoct "fantasy" research findings, and even stoop to bribery.

That's why hearing of an inspirational exception is uplifting to this university professor. It's like throwing open a window so refreshing breezes can rush in, or serendipitously meeting a long-lost, best friend. Why? It restores a small chunk of depleted confidence in humankind's goodness.

An Upstream Swimmer

The veracity of the following story is vouched for by my political science colleague, Joel Fetzer—for it involved *his* major professor at a renown Ivy League school. For starters, this exceptional mentor firmly believed that he best served God by sharing his most valuable insights with promising students. In addition, he coached them until such ideas bore scholarly fruit—appearing polished in prestigious publications. And best of all, he did this quietly and inconspicuously.

Such deeds of extreme generosity are practically unheard of. Research profs, in particular, typically hoard such gems, with the sole intention of using them to advance their own reputations and careers. They galvanize their attention on looking out for numero uno.

Well, a superb idea that this professor shared with a gifted student happened to yield incredibly notable results. In fact, so great was its impact that the student actually ended-up receiving a Nobel Prize! And in his acceptance speech—before the planet's greatest scholars in Sweden—he thoughtfully mentioned his humble and generous professor by name, bestowing him with great honor and gratitude.

The professor had been outed! But after learning what his student had said, predictably, he kept it to himself. It wasn't even divulged to his wife. She was only made aware when, several years later, she accidentally came across a letter quoting the student's magnanimous words.

Some might conclude that the guy should be faulted for being excessively humble, destructively self-effacing, or even masochistic. A cultural maxim maintains that to not be known is, in effect, to not significantly exist. Right? Not even close!

Making P. R. Holy

Her name is Teresa, and even though she had no biological offspring, the world gave her the honorific moniker of *Mother*. She, without a doubt, did innumerable, commendable deeds known only to recipients and to God.

But make no mistake—another part of her was intentionally visible. She actually played to the press—not for personal glory, but to ignite hearts and spur motivations to respond with compassion.

And respond they did. Multitudes contributed money. Others even rearranged priorities to adopt a Teresa-like lifestyle. My friend, Michael Christensen, actually paid his way to India to work beside her and to absorb her passion. He returned to devote a lifetime of selfless, intensive—

but low-profile—charity work and to pen books that inspired others to follow this pathway.

Lady Diana took that same journey to be with the saintly servant. Upon arrival, the English princess was made to wait several hours in a noisy reception room with pathetic, suffering people. The deplorable stench and anguishing sights were light years away from what she was accustomed to—as was her assigned task of administering hands-on care.

Finally, after allowing her to soak up a dose of reality, Mother Teresa appeared to welcome her royal guest. The entire experience left Lady Diana a changed woman. She returned home to invest herself and her resources in charity work in the British Isles. Furthermore, she traveled throughout the world on the mission to rid the world of devastating land mines.

For me, however, one occasion in Mother Teresa's life topped them all. The president of the United States invited this diminutive giant, who had received every humanitarian citation imaginable including the Nobel Prize, to the White House to receive another. In truth, it was our nation being honored by her mere acceptance of the award.

Immediately after stepping off the airplane, she was engulfed and hounded by the press. A limo whisked her away to be welcomed by the first family. Afterward, she was shown to her quarters but, like a squirming kindergartner, refused to stay put. Jet lag? What jet lag?

Those attempting to contact her that afternoon discovered that she was nowhere in sight. But nobody filed a missing person report, for the stalking paparazzi certainly hadn't lost touch with this walking dynamo. They had trailed her to her destination. Halls of Congress? Steps of the Supreme Court? Smithsonian Museum? None of these. Instead, her destination was the poorest section of Washington, D.C.

There she enthusiastically posed for the media and, to their delight, gave in-depth interviews. For her, it was a grandest of opportunities to proclaim her message, namely that the unfortunate deserve our response, and that we who live in the richest nation on earth must become Christ to a broken and destitute world!

She waved her calloused hand and flashed that epic grin for the cameras. Mother Teresa the extrovert, no less! Beaming. Talkative. Demonstrative. Winsome. It was as if she were making a commercial—publicly marketing the eternal rewards of being humanitarian and compassionate!

These are two striking illustrations of persons exemplifying, seemingly, opposite strategies. Joe's professor was intensely secretive. Mother Teresa, at least on the Washington, D.C., occasion, was soliciting attention. Which approach conforms to our Lord's teaching in the Sermon on the Mount? The answer may be surprising. Actually, *both* are right and commendable. To explain, let's briefly revisit the epic sermon.

Inconsistent or Consistent?

We previously concluded that anonymity—grounded in the right motivation—is meritorious and holy (Matthew 6:1-8; 16-18). Our Lord pulled no punches when declaring that our giving, prayer, and fasting should be done for God alone. In reality, Jesus cast an even wider net: "Be careful not to do [any of] your 'acts of righteousness' in front of others, to be seen by them" *(v. 1)*.

In addition to the big three, a plethora of potential acts of righteous showboating rush to mind—any of which can be used for bragging rights: giving "cups of cold water" in Christ's name (10:42), tending to the needs of the "least"—sick, imprisoned, unclothed (25:35-40), loving one's enemies (5:43-48), suffering insult without bitterness (5:12), refusing to worry (6:25-34). Jesus seems to be saying that whatever good deeds we do should be done humbly rather than manifesting a look-at-me-and-eat-your-heart-out demeanor. In reality, the latter is a not-so-subtle put-down to others, while the former elevates the glory of God and insures earthly reward and heavenly treasure (6:19-21).

But if so, how can Mother Teresa's exhibition in our nation's capital be lauded or even justified? Let us once again return to Christ's sermon for the important answer. Paradoxically, the same Lord who advocates secrecy also proclaims the importance of serving God openly and visibly. Let's try to wrap our brains around this truth by contrasting His metaphors of salt and light. He instructed us to be both.

On one hand, His followers are *salt*—seasoning to "bring out the God-flavors of this earth" (5:13 TM). If saltiness is lost, how will people taste godliness?

This clearly refers to an internal, anonymous life that subtly permeates for good. But Jesus also declares that we are to be a beaming, bright *light*:

> You're here to be light, bringing out the God-colors in the world. God is not a secret to be kept. We're going public with this, as public as a city on a hill. If I make you light-bearers, you don't think I'm going to hide you under a bucket, do you? I'm putting you on a light stand. Now that I've put you there on a hilltop on a light stand—shine! Keep open house, be generous with your lives. By opening up to others, you'll prompt people to open up with God, this generous Father in heaven *(5:14-16 TM)*.

What is the source of our light? Jesus declares: "I am the light of the world" (John 9:5). Thus, any shining radiance that we project is a reflection of His light within our hearts—much like Pharos Lighthouse (one of the Seven Wonders of the Ancient World) cast its blazing light 30 miles out to sea with giant mirrors. Like us, it reflected a dazzling light that burned within.

In our modern day it seems that there is no scarcity of light. Even back alleyways and vacant shopping centers glow brightly. In Christ's electricity-deprived day, darkness was everywhere and often dreaded. But then, as well as now, light is a cherished commodity for many reasons. More specifically, when our Lord declares that we are light in the world, what did He likely have in mind? Such light possibly has three crucial purposes:

1. **To be seen.** In His day, when people went out at night, they carried small terracotta lamps filled with olive oil and containing a floating wick. When the light was seen, friends were alerted and enemies were repulsed.

    A secrecy that cowers destroys the potential for discipleship. I once heard about a kid who became a Christian, then went away to work at a summer job. Upon his return a friend asked, "Did the others tease you about your faith?" The boy responded, "I nipped that possibility in the bud early on. I didn't give them the slightest reason to suspect that I was a Christian."

2. **To guide.** When it's dark and the lights go out, even the familiarity with our home isn't enough. If we try to walk around, we're very apt to bump our shin against a piece of furniture or even stumble and fall. That's why we place flashlights and candles in accessible locations.

    We are guiding lights to illuminate the way for those stranded in this world's darkness—pointing them to the true Light of the world.

3. **To warn.** Often a light—usually red—tells us to stop when there is danger ahead. Such is true, for example, for trains speeding headlong toward a collapsed bridge.

    Likewise our prophetic voices must alert people of the results of disobedience. My friend Neil Wiseman passed along a truth when sharing something his father-in-law often declared "Mark my word—sooner or later we must *all* sit down and eat heartily at the *banquet of consequences.*" We must forewarn others of the inevitable consequences of drifting along without God.

The need for salt and light—staples for surviving on earth—is absolutely undeniable. It is also obvious that each has its own unique, vitally important purposes that should parallel intentions of those seeking to live authentic Christian lives. No doubt, that is why our Lord trumpeted these two metaphors. In short, be both the Ivy League professor *and* Mother Teresa.

A Paradox to Embrace

A *conundrum* is loosely defined as something that is puzzling, confusing, or mysterious. On our initial reading of the Sermon on the Mount, some of us may have judged the "secret vs. open" issue to be just that—a conundrum. On one hand, Jesus adamantly instructs followers to be secretive; on the other we're told to "go public."

As we've just concluded, our Lord really meant for us to follow both courses.

Maybe that is a hard pill for us to swallow. We may think we have a real paradox. Why couldn't Jesus have made it more clear—by stating conditions, qualifiers, modifications, or whatever? How can we believe two things that seemingly contradict?

As "children of the Enlightenment," it's our nature to abhor paradoxes. Furthermore, we'll do all within our power to explain them—or explain them away. With our scientific bias, we opt for one interpretation to the exclusion of the other. It has to be either this or that. Period. Then, after deciding, we can place our "chunks" of truth into neat, separate, airtight compartments that correspond with our logic. It's called "having it all figured out."

But for Jesus, paradoxes and the resulting ambiguities they generate, are A-okay. That's why He purposely offers them, forcing us to struggle with the tensions they create. Why must we endure this mental torture? The very process of the ongoing struggle helps us to see deeper, underlying principles far more clearly. The result is that two seemingly inconsistent principles appear increasingly less paradoxical—or not paradoxical at all!

Context: A Key Issue

An absolute necessity for resolving some of the tension lies in investigating contrasting contexts. In particular, we must examine who constitutes the target audience. Let's apply this to the covert vs. overt issue we've been examining.

The do-things-in-secret teaching focuses on the Pharisees, who Matthew's Jewish audience were well aware of. Jesus repeatedly labels them *hypocrites*—fakes, pretenders, and actors intended to be seen and admired. Not incidentally, they were the ones who were our Lord's primary antagonists. Such persons had a major need: to quit showboating their spirituality and stop trying to appear sanctimonious.

Who was the target audience for the counterpart teaching—openly illuminating truth and being involved in public displays of goodness? Here Jesus is presenting himself as the legitimate Messiah to the Jews.

He does this in part by presenting himself as the supreme interpreter of Mosaic Law. Jesus realized that His audience had tremendous respect for the one who led their forefathers out of Egyptian bondage and climbed Mt. Sinai to receive God's instruction for His people. Likewise, our Lord respected Moses—making it crystal clear that He had no wish to obliterate His law (Matthew 5:17).

Although they both went to a mountain, Jesus' teaching did two things to Mosaic law according to my colleague, biblical scholar Ira Jolivet Jr.:

> First, He provided the *intent* behind it. This is exemplified in His teaching on divorce, a concession given by Moses for rare and specific exceptions, to better a deplorable situation. It had become a male "weapon" to jettison a wife for anything that he considered even a minor displeasure.
>
> Second Jesus *closed the loopholes* for using Mosaic law for malevolent purposes such as neglecting the care of their aged parents by claiming they had donated offering to the Temple. Jesus slammed the door on their greedy fingers and articulated the timeless principle of love (Mark 7).

Jesus underscored that He alone is the Messiah, and He instructed this same audience to brightly shine on a hill rather than under a basket Matthew 5:14) for the sole purpose of bringing glory to God. In essence, here is a *new* teaching for God's *new* people, instructing them in how to be faithful people of the *new* covenant.

Understanding the contrasting targeted audiences should wipe away any trace of paradox between secretive, anonymous living and proclaiming widely and loudly the wondrous grace and blessing of God. The message is that if we are ego-driven and playactors by nature, we need a quick trip to our closets and need to keep any good deeds under wraps. If, however, we have a marked tendency to never discuss or display our faith, we are requested to push out into the open by faith; to stand up and be counted.

The unvarnished truth is that we should immerse ourselves in both hidden and open acts of worship. Our lives should balance these two, but not in a mechanical, programmed sense. Relying fully on the trustworthy, inner guidance of God's Spirit, we will know if and when to be involved in which. In His providence, opportunities are bound to continuously present themselves—and if we wander off path, we can trust Him to gently nudge us back on course. When God guides, God provides!

Teeter-tottering

Few would contest that ideally there should be this balance within those of us who consider ourselves disciples of Jesus Christ. At times, however, for good reason we are led by God to excel in one or the other—and rely on others to counterbalance us. Envision a seesaw, the kind you may remember from grammar school. One kid plops his full weight on one end; another does the same on the other end. This weight balance is necessary to make it work.

Not long ago I took my Sociology of Religion class to spend a day and night at Mt. Calvary Monastery that sits high on a Santa Barbara mountain overlooking the Pacific Ocean. Housed at this facility are monks who are called to pray, study, and worship for long hours each day. They live for the most part an inward, inconspicuous, dedicated life of intense reflection and worship. Few know of them or their selfless existence, which, not incidentally, also includes counseling of guests, household duties, and benevolence to the needy in their city.

My friends, the brothers, do most of what they do anonymously—hidden away in that idyllic setting. Their focus is on praying for, supporting, and equipping others who are on the front lines. They're on their end of the seesaw doing their part to balance the multitude who publicly stand tall in the thick of the action.

Charles Swindoll gives us another great illustration of this balance in his book, *Come Before Winter and Share My Hope*. What Howard Hughes and Bill Gates were to the aircraft and computer industries, Martin Luther was to the Protestant Reformation. Hear the courageous words of this mover and shaker: "I am born to fight against innumerable monsters and devils. I must remove stumps and stones, cut away thistles and thorns, and clear the wild forest."

With sweeping statements and incredibly brave actions, this fearless monk of Wittenberg, Germany, awakened saints all across Germany as he fanned the flame of renewal. Rather than causing him to cease and desist, excommunication spurred him on! He needed only God to lean on. Or did he really?

Back in the shadows, hidden behind the charismatic personality of Luther, was another hero—the brains behind the Reformation. Today few Christians would recognize his name. He failed to impress even his biographers. One describes Philip Melancthon as being "of frail body." He had a stammering tongue and one shoulder protruded higher than the other. He did not appear to have the public relations clout to turn heads.

Yet it was this very fellow who exerted the most powerful influence over Luther as the reformer shook his blazing torch in the face of the Church.

- He pioneered the very first Protestant edition of systematic theology.
- He was the genius of the educational systems of Europe, considered the father of modern scholarship.
- His knowledge of New Testament Greek allegedly surpassed that of any other scholar in Europe. That's why Martin continuously consulted him for interpreting difficult passages of Scripture.

The seesaw they rode had near-perfect balance. Luther supplied presence, vigor, and explosive strength. Melancthon chipped in with depth of thought, discretion, and mildness. Luther commended the Reformation to the commoners. But by his gracious low-key moderation, respect for order, and his profound scholarship, Melancthon won over the support of the learned. To sum it up, Luther energized his quiet friend while Melancthon tempered Luther.

When Luther passed away, Melancthon was appropriately chosen to offer the oration. A short time later, the scholar's body was lowered into the same grave—alongside that of the more famous hero of the Reformation. They now rest side by side in the Old Castle Church at Wittenberg. And why not? One was indeed the "wings" of the Reformation; but the other was the "wind beneath those wings."

A Final Word

In this chapter we have attempted to show the great need and legitimacy of both hidden and open discipleship. The former cultivates the spirit, attuning it with that of God; the latter embodies and proclaims the blessed Good News. Indeed, opposite sides of the same Christian coin—or, as someone put it, the holy one-two punch.

Both must be focused on the ultimate goal: bringing glory, praise, and honor to our merciful and mighty God. All falling short of that is totally without merit.

In the next section we will explore seven kinds of immensely rewarding joy that result from living the anonymous Christian life. But for starters, let's briefly examine joy itself. I think of joy as orange in color for some reason: alive, vibrant, and pulsating with brilliance and energy. Bright orange like a Popsicle or a freshly peeled carrot.

Don't expect to read about this spiritual fruit of joy (Galatians 5:6) in a psychology textbook or a philosophy treatise. It belongs entirely in the Christian domain. That's why it shows up nearly 200 times in Scripture. The angels brought *good tidings of great joy* when announcing our Savior's birth (Luke 2:10 KJV). Later, Jesus declared the purpose of His teaching to be *my joy … in you, and … your joy … full* (Jn. 15:11 KJV).

Thus, as Swindoll said, with this incredible gift in our hearts, we shouldn't be "going around looking like our rich aunt just willed her millions to her pregnant hamster!"

Don't confuse joy with *fun,* which you can find at Disneyland or a World Series game. Nor is joy anything like *happiness.* Joy is generated from the wellsprings of our souls when our souls have been touched by God.

For this reason, Christians still have joy when things appear dark, dismal, destitute, and depressing. When fun and happiness beat a hasty exit, joy persists.

Joy adds real zest to our lives. and it is God's free gift to us, even though it cost Him plenty. Joy is something we can possess that makes our lives fulfilling. As I wrote in my book, *Studies in the Sermon on the Mount, Volume 1,* with joy we soar like eagles; without it, we're never more than worms on hang gliders.

Let our minds and hearts be open to His joy as we investigate ways it flows to us when we're content to let Him—and others—receive the credit. Let us be content to receive our reward in a place where neither "moth nor rust destroy, nor thieves break in and steal" (See Matthew 6:19-20).

Discussion Questions:

1. What's your take on Joel's professor? Do you see possible draw-

backs for either the giver or taker in such an arrangement? Can you share similar instances?

2. Are you okay with what Mother Teresa did in Washington, D.C.? What might she have done or said to make it definitely *not* okay?

3. What is there about salt that you can apply to yourself and your witness? How about light? What grade would you give Christians today, in general, for being salt and light? Give your reasons for assigning these grades.

4. In addition to the salt and light paradox, are there others you find to be especially perplexing such as faith and works or God's love and correction? Do such paradoxes create good or bad tension within you?

5. Has there ever been a person in your life who balanced you out as Melancthon did Luther? How about your spouse or a child? In what ways is that stressful? In what ways is it positive?

Action Items

1. You and a friend each make a list of 31 things you could do to bring more kindness into the world. Exchange lists, and each of you do one item each day for a month from the other's list. Keep a journal and share with one another how it went. Don't tell anyone else.

2. Give a tollbooth worker enough money to pay the toll for the car behind you. When explaining this, instruct him or her to hand the driver a note on which you have written *This is to wish you God's best for a great day!*

Section Three

Wondrous Gateway to Immense Joy

Seven
Adoration of the Father
Pure Worship

Chich'en Itza, irreverently pegged "Chicken Pizza" by my students, is located in the northern Yucatan area of Mexico. This pre-Columbian archeological site was once inhabited by the Maya (600-1200 A.D.). Its center is dominated by the Temple of Kukulkan—"feathered serpent" god—which rests atop a gigantic step pyramid.

Accompanied by young anthropology scholars, my wife and I climbed to its zenith. There inside the temple was the ancient Jaguar Throne—a stone altar shaped like the big cat, except that his back was flat to function as a table. Our guide explained that scores of palpitating human hearts, ripped from chests of live people, were placed on this sacred feline's back as offerings to Kukulkan. It was believed that if such grisly sacrifices were not offered frequently, the sun would cease shining, seasons would stop changing, and crops and all human life would perish.

But something else was mentioned that left me perplexed. We were told to take a look at the Jaguar's head, conspicuously turned away from the place of sacrifice. This was a definite indication that Kukulkan possessed a cavalier, stone-cold disinterest in the massive suffering, bleeding, and dying. He was unimpressed.

Don't think of the Maya as lone rangers; most ancient cultures perceived their gods to be impersonal or even antagonistic. It was previously mentioned that the Canaanites considered Baal dispassionate, requiring them to slash their bodies and cry out to get his attention. Greek gods were deemed to possess humanlike frailties and as such were fixated on sensual pursuits rather than assisting or comforting humanity.

Anthropologists reveal that even today scores of isolated tribal cultures possess conceptions of gods that correspond with this same mindset. Pygmies of the Ituri Forest equate their god with the forest and believe he is unconcerned about humans—except to make their hunting unproductive. A month-long song festival, *molimo,* is held to soften his calloused heart. Eskimos of St. Lawrence Island worship Sedna, who lives in the depths of the sea. She has no love for people and seeks to cause them trouble. When her shenanigans become excessive, the witchdoctor dives down to cast his spell. Ojibwa Indians consider their god to be a mystery man who knows many secrets that could greatly benefit people but isn't about to share them. Tribesmen must resort to stealing them by eating hallucinogenic plants and having visions.

How do humans typically relate to deities they consider so remote, unfeeling, and mean-spirited? They attempt to alert, arouse, or appease them. But in doing so, their only goal is to survive—*not* to initiate or expect intimacy, companionship, or comfort. Most would consider that to be abhorrently out of line, enough to incur the gods' immediate, harsh punishment.

Without a glimmer of hope of their gods offering even a semblance of loving kindness, such folks consider themselves to be on their own in a threatening world. For them life is little more than a lonely, tooth-and-claw existence.

"God-cepts" Today

In ancient civilizations, as well as in backward cultures today, the incredible privilege of knowing the true, Judeo-Christian God of the

Bible is missing. Today you and I have been made aware of Him through sermons, books, films, testimonies, and even personal revelation. Our perception of God should be in sharp contrast to that of ancient or backward cultures. But is it?

In his captivating book *Your God Is Too Small,* respected author and Bible translator J. B. Phillips thinks not. He concludes that all too often we succumb to forming spurious images corresponding with our personal desires. Those images bear no resemblance to the God of the Bible.

Specifically, like those we've discussed, our "god-cepts" fashion God as uncaring or hostile. As a result, when things go really sour, we're tempted to be angry toward the God-caricatures we've created in our minds. Phillips spells out some of these glaring misconceptions of God that are popular today even among believers. Here is his take on how God is often seen today:

God is a resident policeman. He is a killjoy, ready to pounce on us when we mess up by making us feel miserable and guilty. The result is that it's difficult to lovingly serve such a nagging robber of pleasure.

God is a grand old gentleman. He's old-fashioned, in keeping with the ancient Jews and the Early Church, and irrelevant today. The result is that while we respect the dear old fellow, we don't expect Him to supply meaning for the present. He's outdated, and His message is archaic.

God is a heavenly aspirin tablet. He sedates us when we're overwhelmed by problems so we no longer feel pressure or pain. This results in our using God as a means of escape, childish regression, and prolonged and enhanced emotional immaturity.

God is a celestial computer. He's the steadying force but is totally preoccupied with keeping the universe running smoothly. The result is that He's seen as unconcerned about relating to us as individuals.

God is the candy man. He makes everything tantalizing and delicious, satiating our sugarcoated cravings. If we opt for this image, we'll inevitably reap bitter disappointment.

Rejecting Distortion to Embrace Accuracy

As we've intimated, the disparity between these perceptions and the God of Abraham couldn't be more vivid or conclusive. So let's set the record straight. To begin with, it's imperative that we understand and embrace our Heavenly Father's *natural attributes*. Four primary ones are as follows:

1. He is eternal. "Lord, you have been our dwelling place throughout all generations. Before the mountains were born or you brought forth the earth and the world, from everlasting to everlasting you are God" (Psalm 90:1-2).

2. He is unchangeable. "You remain the same, and your years will never end" (Hebrews 1:12).

3. He is all-wise. "Oh, the depth of the riches of the wisdom and knowledge of God! How unsearchable his judgments, and his paths beyond tracing out!" (Romans 11:33).

4. He is all-powerful. "With man this is impossible, but with God all things are possible" (Matthew 19:26).

To even partially wrap our minds around these attributes is to provide us with a sense of well-being and security. We can rest assured that the God we serve isn't some erratic heavenly being fraught with glaring weaknesses, out-of-control passions, and continuous inconsistencies. Rather, He is stable and stalwart. As a result, our glorious, eternal Creator saturates our very existence with meaning, purpose, and confidence—despite Satan's disruptive schemes. We enthusiastically concur with those who proclaim that God is in His heaven and all is right with the world!

As refreshing as these natural attributes are to contemplate, a rehearsal of God's moral characteristics may be even more assuring, because they have a direct bearing on how we relate to our Creator. Combined, they certainly fly in the face of anyone concluding that He is oblivious or mean-spirited. Let's look more closely at four of His moral characteristics.

1. He is just. "Surely God does not reject a blameless man or strengthen the hands of evildoers" (Job 8:20).

2. He is holy. "The LORD said to Moses, 'Speak to the entire assembly of Israel and say to them: "Be holy because I, the LORD your God, am holy"'" (Leviticus 19:2-1).

3. He is merciful. "As high as the heavens are above the earth, so great is his love for those who fear him" (Psalm 103:11).

4. He is loving. "Whoever does not love does not know God, because God is love" (1 John 4:8).

The fact could not be more emphatically revealed: Our Heavenly Father cares deeply, continuously and consistently, even about the smallest detail of our lives. Period. Case closed. Without a doubt, this is a dominant, underscored theme in Scripture. But might there be a single biblical teaching that ties a ribbon around all four of His moral characteristics? Absolutely. Read on.

A Quintessential Title

In the Sermon on the Mount, Jesus entreats His disciples to pray "Our Father in heaven" (Matthew 6:9). Many of us are accustomed to non-reflectively launching into the Lord's Prayer with these words.

However, comprehending God as Father was exceedingly revolutionary to our Lord's followers. That's why German theologian Joachim Jeremias concludes it was, arguably, Christ's greatest revelation—with crucial implications. Neither his listeners nor their ancestors had ever pictured God in such an intimate manner. Instead, their prophets had instructed them to envision Him as high and lofty, holy and immortal.

But suddenly Jesus, who knows God best, in effect asks His disciples to imagine all the best love of the best fathers who ever lived. Paul picks up on this marvelous fatherhood imagery:

> You did not receive a spirit that makes you a slave again to fear, but you received the Spirit of sonship. And by him we cry, "Abba, Father." The Spirit himself testifies with our spirit that we are God's

children. Now if we are children, then we are heirs—heirs of God and co-heirs with Christ, if indeed we share in his sufferings in order that we may also share in his glory *(Romans 8:15-17)*.

What about this term, *Abba*? Put simply, it is Hebrew for *Da-da*. Jesus is telling us to address the infinite, majestic, all-powerful God with Hebrew baby talk! *Abba* is how a Jewish toddler addressed the one who picked him or her up, hugged him or her tightly, kissed his or her cheek, and dangled a colorful toy. Informality, warmth, and deep affection are all implied.

The *Abba* idea gives everything a new slant and feel. Fear and worry are replaced with faith and trust. Indeed, fear no longer computes. As Brennan Manning states in his book *Abba's Child*, "We live in the wisdom of accepted tenderness."

Intense Care and Intimacy

Does the concept of *Abba* seem to share common ground with an impersonal or deviously antagonistic deity? Obviously not, so we can relax in His presence, knowing that He can be trusted to supply our basic needs: food aplenty, as He furnishes for the birds (see Matthew 6:26) and clothes for our bodies, just as He adorns forest wildflowers (vv. 28-29).

Furthermore our *Abba* gives attention to the slightest details of our lives, down to a precise inventory of the hairs on our heads (Matthew 10:30). Like a responsible Father, He lovingly monitors us closely at all times, even when we're totally unaware.

Never Found in a Box Seat!

In His Sermon on the Mount, Jesus proclaims that God relishes anonymous acts of love directed toward Him. Good deeds—almsgiving, prayer, fasting—are commendable, but only if their primary, underlying intention is to glorify our blessed Lord. When done with that as motive, in a very real sense they are true acts of worship.

In contrast, doing good to impress others so they'll consider us devoted, meritorious, or holy is detestable to Him. Let's retrace our steps to the mountain and allow Christ's words in Matthew 6 to provide a take on God's preference for us.

> Be especially careful when you are trying to be good so that you don't make a performance out of it. It might be good theater, but the God who made you won't be applauding (v. 1, TM).

> When you help someone out don't think about how it looks. Just do it—quietly and unobtrusively. That is the way your God, who conceived you in love, working behind the scenes, helps you out. And when you come before God, don't turn that into a theatrical production either. All these people making a regular show out of their prayers, hoping for stardom! Do you think God sits in a box-seat? Here's what I want you to do: Find a quiet, secluded place so you won't be tempted to role-play before God. Just be there as simply and honestly as you can manage. The focus will shift from you to God, and you will begin to sense his grace (vv. 4-6, TM).

> When you practice some appetite-denying discipline to better concentrate on God, don't make a production out of it. It might turn you into a small-time celebrity but it won't make you a saint. If you "go into training" inwardly, act normal outwardly (vv. 16-18, TM).

Showboating our piety before others will not earn us special recognition from them or God. It's definitely counterproductive when it comes to our *Abba*. A positive, humble, overt witness is crucially important. However, if done to enhance our egos or to score points, potential good is erased. To help us avoid falling into these ditches, God plainly and simply states His strong preference for behind-the-scenes, inconspicuous deeds of goodness and intimate communion in a quiet and secluded location.

To some degree, we are all prone to vanity. But Jesus declared that "Whoever wants to become great among you must be your servant, and whoever wants to be first must be your slave—just as the Son of Man did not come to be served, but to serve" (Matthew 20:26-28).

Servants and slaves don't grab spotlights. Their work is strictly behind the scenes. Their primary goal is to please their masters, to conform to their wishes.

Furthermore, their entire reason for being would be severely diminished or completely obliterated by stealing the limelight. Can you imagine a state governor's wardrobe assistant hearing the press ask the governor an important question and seizing the microphone to respond?

How much more than any politician is our God entitled to be the center of attention! As His faithful servants, we're to be obedient to His commandments and faithful to do what He has asked us to do. Our joy is derived from glorifying the Master.

We must have much the same attitude as John the Baptist when, prior to baptizing our Lord in the Jordan River, he proclaimed to the crowd, "He must become greater, I must become less" (John 3:30).

As mortals with limited perspective, we wonder how our Heavenly Father, so great, mighty, and intelligent, could desire closeness with lowly, sin-prone humans such as us. What of value can we possibly offer Him? Evidently, He yearns simply for the warmth of our fellowship and devotion. Our very presence, especially when shared by just Him and us, brings joy to His loving heart.

Discussion Questions:

1. Have you encountered or heard about any ancient or contemporary cultures that believe God is remote or mean-spirited? Share.

2. Focusing on J. B. Phillips' five popular misconceptions of God today, do you know of someone who seems to concur with any or all of the five? Have you ever been tempted to embrace any of the five? What were the consequences?

3. Once we fully believe in the four natural attributes of God mentioned in this chapter, what difference does that make in our lives? How about His four moral characteristics?

4. Do you warm up to the idea of truly considering the God of the universe as your *Abba*? Why or why not? What are the practical consequences of this belief?

Action Items

1. Engage in a worthwhile volunteer activity with likeminded persons who will intentionally refrain from seeking credit. Remember: this is a "we" project rather than a "me" project.

2. When receiving a compliment or reward, purposely defer the accorded honor to another or others who have made their contributions behind the scenes.

Eight
Heaven's Treasure Chest
Anticipated Reward

She looked destitute and pathetic sitting on the park bench. Next to her were two plastic bags jammed full of her stuff. The spectacle of her shoddy appearance, mussed hair, and shabby clothing prompted both pity and laughter from passersby. She apparently had nowhere to go when the weather turned inclement and lacked the wherewithal to survive outdoors.

The passing traffic didn't seem to faze her. Day after day she just sat there, not looking up when teenagers yelled at her as they drove past. She was alone.

Not knowing her personally, people drew their own sordid conclusions. The rumor mill did its work. Some surmised that her house had burned down; others concluded she was drug addict. Still others thought she had a mental condition and were afraid to get too close. Most everyone described her with uncomplimentary labels—"vagrant," "vagabond," "drifter," "tramp."

What was her real story? What had she been previously? How did she sink to this deplorable condition? Most important, what options and resources could she use to rehabilitate herself? Was her situation hopeless?

When she died, few took more than passing notice as they hurried by her former home on the bench. One reporter, however, decided to get to the bottom of her life and write an in-depth biography. He discovered that, as conjectured, she suffered from mental health issues and had been victimized by crises.

However, by far the most significant fact he uncovered was that she was extremely wealthy. As it turns out, she was one of the most affluent homeless women on record. Her carefully hidden stash was discovered in the lining of her clothes and inside her mattress.

What had blocked this tortured soul from enjoying a comfortable, even luxurious, material existence? While other factors undoubtedly contributed, it seems the greatest culprit was her miserly spirit. She was a tightwad who scrimped and saved and hoarded her last penny.

She evidently loved money, and she delighted in clutching it tightly. Maybe it provided her with a strange sense of security, or maybe she imagined how impressive it would be to have the last laugh on all those who had deemed her a worthless pauper.

The key details of this story were pieced together from what I recall hearing as a child. Surprisingly, many I've shared it with say they've heard similar stories.

I find it significant that this perplexing lady had directed her time, energy, talents, and possessions toward one goal—a twisted kind of self-fulfillment. She apparently sought rewards from neither people in this life nor God in the next. Granted, she carried out her own agenda anonymously—but with the wrong motive.

A Look at Contrasts

Let's contrast the self-directed reward, to which this woman aspired, with that of three kinds of people.

Rewards on Earth

First, there are those who play to the crowd to obtain highly conspicuous rewards on earth: wealth, position, acclaim. These people crave applause, favors, or the adoring strokes of others.

According to Jesus, such persons receive their rewards in the here and now. (See Matthew 6:2, 5, 16.) This negates receiving eternal reward from God in heaven. As we all know, any material bounty that accompanies earthly notoriety isn't transferable. Shrouds have no pockets, and U-haul trucks never follow hearses to the cemetery. What's amassed on earth stays on earth.

Rewards on Earth and in Heaven Simultaneously

Many wish to earn rewards on earth and in heaven simultaneously. As with financial wizards on Wall Street, their investments are intended to reap short- as well as long-term profits. Not content for merely pie-in-the-sky-by-and-by, they scramble for tangible benefits in this life as well. If one's good, both must be better.

I remember an incident that occurred some years ago. My late mother, a nurse, had heard the impassioned appeal of a missionary doctor who spoke at her church. He described being so limited in equipment that he resorted to using razor blades in place of scalpels. Mom's heartstrings were plucked, and she responded with a sizeable contribution.

Then she did something I don't recall her ever doing before. She let others know of her generosity. Predictably, she was showered with compliments, which she seemed to relish.

I decided to have a bit of fun with her. "Mom, you know, don't you, that all that money you gave will net you zero in heaven? You blew it by bragging to your friends." With a big smile she retorted, "Son, I've done a slew of anonymous things in my life, all to the glory of God—enough to have stored up quite a stockpile in heaven. I figured I could afford to get a little credit on earth." I dropped it.

Only His Reward

Third, there are folks in this category who, without others being aware, live and give to God alone. For them, it's only His reward that matters. These are the holy anonymous our Lord highly commends. (See Matthew 6.) Theirs is not a quid pro quo, I'll-scratch-your-back-if-you'll-scratch-mine, expectation. Rather, it's based solely on the motive of love.

According to Jesus, this kind of person doesn't merely earn additional heavenly gingerbread. Matthew 7:21 tells us that it's imperative that we seek to obey God if we're to gain entry into His eternal kingdom. Prophesying, casting out devils, and other noble works are, alone, insufficient. Truly obeying God means giving and faithfully serving Him in secret.

Let's pause to consider an issue that's basic to this discussion. It focuses on the legitimacy of being motivated by any rewards whatsoever.

Is Reward Talk Really "Christian"?

Some maintain that consideration of reward—even heaven—has no legitimate place in the believer's mind or life. God's disciples should be good for the mere sake of being good. After all, as they say, virtue is its own reward.

But three times Jesus speaks of reward in the Sermon on the Mount—in regard to almsgiving, prayer, and fasting—and on plenty of other occasions too. Here is a sampling of things for which believers receive heavenly reward:

- Matthew 5:12—bearing persecution and suffering insult without bitterness
- Matthew 10:42—giving a person a cup of cold water
- Matthew 25:14-30—faithful service
- Matthew 25:31-46—responding to the needs of others

We must not disregard the importance of rewards as we align our priorities and sharpen our focus to correspond with those of the Lord. Rewards provide us with valuable goals that we joyfully pursue. And they remind us that we serve a just God who truly cares about our following the pathway of goodness and obedience. How do we know that? Because that's what He promises to reward us for. Consider two essential things we should keep in mind when reflecting on the reward Jesus alludes to.

Spiritual reward transcends the material. Admittedly, in many places throughout the Old Testament, prosperity and material gain were closely connected. The predominant purpose of the Book of Job seems to lay this notion to rest, however.

Christian reward is elusive. Paradoxically, reward comes to ones who do not seek it. If we constantly calculate what rewards we're earning, we're likely to see God as a judge or accountant and life in terms of *law*. The thinking goes, "It's mine—I've earned it, I'm entitled!" If we aren't given it, we complain that we've been wronged.

Authentic Christian reward is not cast in this manner. Rather, it predominantly frames all in terms of *love*. When we're in a love relationship with Christ, we're far more likely to focus on what we owe Him rather than carefully calculating any reward to which we feel entitled. As a result, our attention is on giving rather than receiving. That's what God's grace is all about!

Perks He Slips In

As Christians, our eyes are fixed on eternal reward. Our single, greatest ambition is to one day hear our Heavenly Father say, "Well done, good and faithful servant; thou has been faithful over a few things, I will make thee ruler over many things: enter thou into the joy of thy lord" (Matthew 25:23, KJV).

Nevertheless, as William Barclay alludes to in his commentary *The Gospel of Matthew, Volume 1*, derivative blessings in this life come to those who are spiritually minded and not motivated by material things:

- satisfaction and inner peace
- increasing responsibility
- a clearer vision of God

This all adds up to a life of joy. That joy is a wellspring within the soul that continues to flow in spite of adversity.

What about those who lock their attention on the rewards of this life? It seems that the more they acquire, the more they desire. The very act of acquiring more becomes their treasure.

The Lord had a lot to say about the futility and foolishness of opting for rewards in this life.

Here Today, Gone Tomorrow

Barclay goes on to examine Matthew 6:19-21, in which Jesus candidly provides three reasons earthly treasures aren't worthy of our primary attention.

They are vulnerable to being eaten by moths. The primary reference here is to clothes. At some point, all clothes hit the closet, and that's where little critters begin their hearty feast. Have you ever pulled out a favorite wool sweater and found those unsightly holes in it?

They are prone to another kind of eating away. The Greek word used for this is translated "rust." Likely, the reference is to rats, mice, worms, and other vermin invading and consuming grain, threatening our food supply.

Finally, all valued earthly treasures are subject to being stolen by thieves. In Palestine, walls of many houses were made of baked clay. Burglars easily dug through walls and seized all they desired. Today, in spite of high-tech alarm systems and guard dogs, thieves still succeed in invading homes and leaving with their victims' belongings.

This all goes to prove that the things of this world are temporary, in stark contrast to our heavenly reward, which is eternal and permanent.

We are in transit to a better place, destined to land eventually on a glorious "distant shore." And upon arrival our reward awaits us.

Down deep we know these things. So why isn't heaven more dominant in our thinking? Why doesn't its reality condition everything we think, do, and feel? Why are so many of us mesmerized by temporary and corruptible treasures? The answer is closely related to the reasons we're less prone to live anonymously for God.

Tripped-up by Diversions and Deceptions

Because we live in an up-close-and-personal world, we rarely ponder our heavenly home. It seems so distant, and our vision of heaven is fuzzy and distorted.

As for our going there, many of us believe that when the time comes, God will wink at our sins and allow us to enter. We have adopted the Hollywood view of heaven, believing that the dearly departed invariably enter the golden gates in style and immediately become involved in doing all their favorite things.

Finally, generally speaking, most of us resist the thought of delayed gratification. Perhaps it's because technology has afforded us instant everything—photos, communication, food.

Conversely, one of the most dreaded words in our vocabulary is *wait*. Our culture is saturated with Type A personalities darting past on highways. They crowd in line at the supermarkets, climbing over any person or obstacle that might slow them down.

So it stands to reason that if we're obsessed with this life's rewards and lack a clear vision of heaven, we're not likely to invest ourselves in laying up treasures where moths and rust do not corrupt.

There is a striking disinterest in heaven—not just among nonbelievers but also among affluent North American Christians. In an off-handed remark, Arthur Ingler nailed the underlying reason: Most of us believers have it too good to think about—much less yearn for—that "pearly white city." More than previous generations, we're showered with an abundance of earthly comforts and know little of life-threatening persecution that still exists elsewhere.

The result is that few of us feel as if we're strangers, pilgrims, or aliens, which were biblical descriptors our predecessors closely identified with. We're far more likely to feel as if we're managers or stockholders, more settlers than drifters. Our roots are deep, and our investments in the here-and-now are considerable.

Could it be that many of us might consider a summons to be with Jesus in the indescribable home He has been preparing for us for 2,000 years to be a rather unwelcome intrusion into our busy schedules?

For many believers, indulging in excessive, or even minimal, thoughts of heaven implies escapism, detachment with the present, and being uselessly visionary.

Reality Check Time

There's a good reason why heaven is spoken of no fewer than 582 times in 505 different verses in God's Word. Our hearts should melt and our hopes soar with inspiration and gratitude when we read triumphant words such as "Our citizenship is in heaven. And we eagerly await a Savior from there, the Lord Jesus Christ, who, by the power that enables him to bring everything under his control, will transform our lowly bodies so that they will be like his glorious body" (Philippians 3:20-21).

In the grand scheme of things, life passes in the blink of an eye and, compared to heaven, is an inconsequential and fleeting moment in time. I was vividly reminded of how brief our appointed time on earth is as I gazed at the Great Wall of China and the Egyptian pyramids, both standing in splendor for 3,000 years

Joni Eareckson Tada notes in her book *Heaven: Your Real Home* that the slogan "Slow down and live" appears on everything from highway signs to health books. But time has a mind of its own, and we're helpless in trying to decrease its velocity. Applying wrinkle cream, pumping bran and brawn with vitamins E and A, and even freezing the body in a hydrogen chamber won't do it. Steadily and consistently, time proceeds ahead, pulling us in tow. Like it or not, these hearts of ours beat like muffled drums, in steady cadence, as we march to our graves.

Joy Unspeakable

Anticipation of our heavenly reward yields abundant joy. Our Father and His Son are waiting to welcome us, as are scores of our brothers and sisters in Christ. It will be party time!

We'll encounter angels and unimaginable surroundings, mansions for everyone, a crystal sea, gates of pearl, walls of precious gems, and gold so plentiful that it's used to pave the roads!

As Joni Eareckson Tada likes to say, "It's the land of 'no-mores.'" You'll find them listed in Revelation 21:4: No more sorrow, no more mourning, no more crying, no more pain, no more death. Everything we love, value—everything of eternal worth—is in heaven.

Jesus says we have a choice. We can either lay up corruptible treasures on earth by doing good in order to be seen and rewarded by people, or we can gain eternal treasure in heaven by doing good in secret for our Heavenly Father.

Discussion Questions

1. Thinking about the park bench lady, have you ever misjudged another by focusing on that person's appearance and demeanor? Any tips on how we might avoid doing this?

2. Describe someone you've encountered who seemed to have a cavalier or blasé idea of heaven. What might have prompted it? What difference did it make in his or her life?

3. To what extent are we tempted to mistakenly conclude that exhibited or publicized good works and ethical deeds are transferable to heaven?

4. What do you make of the statement "Christian reward is elusive—paradoxically coming to ones who do not purposely seek it"?

5. What diversions and deceptions sometimes prohibit you from contemplating the glories of your future life in heaven?

Action Items

1. Take some time to visit with an older Christian who has many friends and family in heaven. Listen intently as he or she describes some very special persons he or she is eager to meet again.

2. Set aside time to search the Scriptures for verses pertaining to heaven. Journal your thoughts, and share them with another.

Nine
From Success to Significance
Authenticity

I heard the story of a very poor boy who, working as a door-to-door salesman to pay his university tuition, became famished but realized he was down to his last dollar. Swallowing his pride, he decided to ask for a bite from the next house he came to. An elegant lady opened the door. He suddenly became so nervous that he could manage only to request a glass of water.

She sensed his need and instead brought a large, cold glass of milk. After slowly drinking it, he asked, "How much is that?"

"You owe me nothing," replied the lady. She added, "My mother taught me never to accept anything in return for an act of kindness."

Years later the same woman became very ill. She was taken to a hospital in a large city nearby. Oddly enough, that same young boy had become a doctor. More astonishing still, he was assigned to her case. When he saw her name on the chart, he realized immediately who she was. He introduced himself to her, and she was overjoyed.

After a long and arduous health battle, she recovered, whereupon the doctor requested the bill be sent to him for approval. He revised it and signed it, then attached a note to her invoice. The lady had worried that it would take the rest of her life to pay her huge medical bill. Excited to be healthy again yet worried about the cost, she reluctantly opened the envelope. To her amazement and delight the note read: *This bill was paid some years ago with a glass of milk.*

Happenstance? Fluke? Proof that everything that goes around *always* comes around? She chose to believe it was simply a beautiful response made possible by unique, providential circumstances to a small gesture of kindness. But the impact on both of them was great.

Granted, neither action was strictly anonymous. They were aware of each other's kindness; plus, in the second instance, workers in the hospital's billing office realized what had taken place. But that's where it ended. The lady didn't proclaim the merits of her gift to the young man to her neighbors or church friends. Likewise, the doctor refrained from peddling news of his benevolence for personal or professional advantage. Their motives were identical—to lovingly extend a helping hand without expecting any notoriety or return.

These two persons chose to engage in truly significant actions. For Christians, *significance* implies being appreciatively more compassionate, honest, humble, and generous than anyone has reason to expect us to be.

To begin unpacking the rich treasure trove of significance, let's examine the four levels of significance outlined by Stephen Covey in his book *The 7 Habits of Highly Effective Families.*

Stairway to the Top

The bottom level is *survival.* Many of us literally fight for it—not just economically but also mentally, spiritually, and socially. Our lives are saturated with uncertainty and fear. We scramble just to make it through the day.

Recently a tragic report focused on the economic hardships of many elderly Americans living alone on fixed income. It was reported that on many days they have to decide whether to eat or purchase badly needed medication. Theirs is a world of dire need and uncertainty. They're victimized by circumstance or outright injustice.

Some of us may have the wherewithal to rise above survival mode, but we choose to remain there. We may fear taking risks necessary for potential advancement, or we may opt for a crippling dependency—choosing to freeload off others while abrogating responsibility for self-improvement. In all of these cases we're locked into a very difficult, marginal existence—mostly living from day to day and hand to mouth.

Level two is *stability.* This is when much of our uncertainty is quelled and our sense of desperation isn't quite as intense. Perhaps we've honed our limited survival skills. We may even have brief respites from feeling completely drained and destitute. We feel that things have leveled off a tad and that life is cutting us a little slack. But our paramount day-to-day goal is still to sustain ourselves. We're still dogged with the thought that even a slight turn for the worse would land us back on level one, where we would then feel even more hopeless and helpless than before.

Level three is *success.* When we attain goals that elevate our perceived importance within our culture, we've taken a bite from that golden apple of success. In practical terms, it means possessing power (having commands obeyed and wishes granted), privilege (being given special rights or favors), and/or possessions (accumulating property and financial security).

Successful people are said to have it made. This perception is enhanced by designer clothing, eating in exquisite restaurants, or driving luxury cars. Make no mistake—who we are perceived to be really does make a huge difference. Just ask Paul Byrd.

A premium pitcher for the Cleveland Indians, Byrd shares a humorous story. It was peak tourist season when he once visited Boston. Upon arrival, he repeatedly tried without success to get dinner reservations at several nice restaurants, but at each restaurant he called he was curtly told that there were no tables available.

Then a mischievous idea hit him. Paul's father was named Larry, so Paul phoned back and said, "Larry Byrd asked me to call and reserve one of your finest tables." The first place he called gave him a reservation.

Although their last names were spelled differently, Larry Bird—former Hall of Fame NBA player for the Boston Celtics—had exalted celebrity status in Boston. This meant he could have *any* reservation *anywhere* for the asking.

Success is society telling us we've arrived, then treating us as if they actually believe it. That's why so many of us are success-obsessed.

Reaching the Top

The fourth and highest level is *significance*. Significance is, in the final essence, what makes life truly worthwhile. And having it gives us joy. This is what George Bernard Shaw said in *Man and Superman: A Comedy and a Philosophy*—

> **This is the one true joy in life,** the being used for a purpose recognized by yourself as a mighty one; the being a force of nature instead of a feverish, selfish clod of ailments and grievances, complaining that the world will not devote itself to making you happy.
>
> I am of the opinion that my life belongs to the whole community, and as long as I live it is my privilege to do for it whatever I can. I want to be thoroughly used up when I die, for the harder I work the more I live.
>
> I rejoice in life for its own sake. Life is no "brief candle" to me. It is a sort of splendid torch which I have got hold of for the moment, and I want to make it burn as brightly as possible before handing it on to future generations *(emphasis added)*.

Significance bears down on the crucial question "When all is said and done, what does it all mean anyhow?" According to author Gail Sheehy, author of *Passages: Predictable Crises of Adult Life,* in our 30s and 40s we're typically busting ourselves to attain success. We surround ourselves with the toys of affluence and key components of future security. We rush to get our ducks in a row before age creeps up on us and opportunity fades.

But then in our late 40s or early 50s, the period of the so-called midlife crisis, after we've attained a measure of financial security and our offspring are making it fine, we begin to engage in some heavy-duty introspection. We ask such questions as—

> Are my priorities aligned with my best interests and/or God's will, or am I just treading water, involved with things of little consequence?
>
> If I should die now, what will be my legacy? How will I be remembered?
>
> How can I utilize my time, effort, and resources in the best possible way?

But my question is this: Why must we wait until late middle age to confront our significance? Why not begin the noble voyage of its attainment in our youth? Life is cumulative. As I've heard many times, *thought leads to action, action to habit, and habit to destiny.* So what's to stop us from thinking about it early on?

Andrew K. Benton, the president of Pepperdine University, agrees. He confronts graduation classes with words that approximate these: "I have little doubt that you students, so well-prepared and so gifted with intelligence, will achieve success. My only concern is that, along with that success, you will be certain to grasp true significance."

Significance isn't always born out of success. It can spring from either the survival or stability levels. The simple fact is that we can inject life with meaning and highly significant acts even if we're destitute.

Significant for What and Whom?

Granted, the authentic life lived significantly is very attractive and appealing. We want what we do to make a difference in the world.

But even the achievement of significance isn't always cause for admiration. Serial killers desiring to see their names in bold headlines achieve a measure of it. The southern California arsonist who eagerly anticipates surging Santa Ana winds to fan his flames realizes a twisted kind of significance.

Also, non-malevolent persons involved with pursuits that only they care about attain valuable, personal meaning—even those who have off-the-wall but innocent hobbies like me. Nobody clamors to view my collection of labeled rocks from places such as the Great Wall of China, Valley of the Kings, and Capernaum. For that matter, I probably couldn't pay anyone to feign interest in my autographed major league baseballs, even though I paid dearly for some of them.

Another important fact: significance does not require longevity. This is especially true in regard to spur-of-the-moment, "random" acts of kindness we perform.

What each of us finds significant varies widely. With that in mind, we're well-advised to galvanize attention on what God considers significant. The greatest significance we can ever hope to achieve is the knowledge that we're authentically pleasing to Him.

This kind of anonymous living is bound to yield a deep sense of significance accompanied by inner jubilation. Why? Unlike a life that seeks only to evoke applause, such a life is far less impacted by negative feedback. Sure, when others relish taking pot shots at us, it has an effect. We're never totally immune from the pain that accompanies being attacked. However, we won't be put out of commission; the wounds will heal, and our faith in our Healer and Helper will intensify.

Indeed, being a slave to public opinion can be inconvenient and annoying. But for some, it's downright devastating. In 1986 the Los Angeles Angels played in the American League Championship series. Their opponent was the Boston Red Sox. Cowboy film star and Angels' owner Gene Autry was up in years, and everyone was very hopeful to present the greatly loved celebrity with a championship.

It was October 12, the day of game number five. At the time the Angels held a three-games-to-one lead in a best-of-seven series. At a very crucial time in the match, relief pitcher Donnie Ray Moore was brought in from the bullpen. He needed just one more strike to clinch the team's first-ever pennant. David Henderson was Boston's batter. Here's the actual transcript of the play-by-play by announcer Al Michaels:

> The pitch. Deep to left, and Downing goes back. And it's gone! Unbelievable! You're looking at one for the ages here. Astonishing! Anaheim Stadium was one strike away from turning into Fantasyland! And now the Red Sox lead 6-5!

Henderson had stomped on the fans' dream by clobbering this "round-tripper." The fans were livid, depressed, and shocked. And, as fans tend to do, they took it out on the pitcher. To compound the grief, the Sox went on to win the remaining games and advance to the World Series.

Moore, who had long battled depression, was dealt a severe mental blow by this event. He began a downward spiral that ended in his abrupt release from baseball. But neither he nor the fans could wipe the traumatic event from memory. Neither forgot. Neither forgave.

On July 18, 1989, all the repercussions of the 1986 loss—the decline and end of his baseball career and serious marital and financial difficulties—along with his battle with alcoholism, drug abuse, and severe depression, finally overcame the pitcher. During an argument with his wife, Tonya, Moore shot her three times in front of their three children. Then, Moore, age 35, shot himself. Unlike his wife, he died.

Never underestimate the power of a high-profile event, especially for those who consider their primary significance in crowd approval. It's strictly a win-all-or-lose-all proposition. There's no in-between. Donnie discovered this the hard way.

But not so for those of us who consider our significance to be anchored in God. As long as with His assistance and guidance we're seeking to make a difference for good, not for the approval of others but for His approval alone, we possess the joy of authentic significance.

From Moore to Mordecai

For Donnie Moore, significance was about winning and earning the fans' approval. When his career went south, his sense of significance plummeted. Compounding other negatives in his life, the net result was tragic.

Contrast Donnie Moore's life with that of Mordecai, a man whose life is portrayed in the Book of Esther. He lived around 460 B.C. in the Persian city of Susa, where King Xerxes had his palace. Mordecai happened to be a member of the Jewish community, which had been captured and exiled to this distant land.

Queen Vashti "defiled" her husband by refusing his demand to parade her beauty before himself and his friends. This made him livid, and taking the advice of a top confidant, he decided to trash his defiant, disrespectful wife and find another.

The search for a new queen led to Mordecai's house, where he lived with his stunningly beautiful cousin, Esther. She was promptly chosen as a finalist and transported to the palace where, along with her competitors, she began a 12-month regimen of high-quality food and luxurious beauty treatments. When King Xerxes saw her, he was smitten and chose her as his queen. But Esther refrained from revealing her Jewish identity.

Meanwhile, Mordecai spent his time sitting at the king's gate—close enough to keep tabs on his cousin's welfare. While there, he happened to overhear two army officers plotting to assassinate the king. He shared this with Esther, who passed it along to Xerxes, giving proper credit to Mordecai. The two conspirators were hanged.

Problems began when Xerxes appointed Haman as chief noble and commanded all to bow down when he passed by. Mordecai refused, and Haman became enraged, especially after learning that Mordecai was Jewish. Haman scurried to Xerxes to convince him that all Jews were troublemakers and should be wiped out. The king agreed and gave Haman his own signet ring to seal the deal.

When Mordecai heard about this decree, he put on sackcloth and ashes and proceeded into the city, wailing. Esther learned of her cousin's anguish and was distressed. She sent clothes to him to replace his sackcloth, hoping that might cheer him up, but he refused to wear them.

Esther then sent a servant to learn what he could. Mordecai explained everything to the servant and told him to urge Esther to go to the king and beg for mercy. She balked, however, fearing that such a bold move would threaten her own life. When Mordecai learned of her reluctance, he sent back this stern response:

> Do not think that because you are in the king's house you alone of all the Jews escape. For if you remain silent… you and your father's family will perish. And who knows but that you have come to royal position for such a time as this? *(Esther 4:12-14)*.

The queen was convinced. She instantly vowed that if all Jews would fast for her for three days, she would approach the king. Then she added, "And if I perish, I perish" (v. 16).

But she didn't perish. The king was delighted that she came, especially after she invited him and Haman to a banquet she would prepare. In gratitude, he invited her to make any request—up to half of his kingdom. She preferred to take a rain check, replying that she would plan to make such a request at her banquet.

Meanwhile, Mordecai again refused to bow down when Haman approached the king's gate. As before, Haman seethed with rage. His wife, Zeresh, and friends impulsively advised him to build a gallows and ask the king to have Mordecai hanged on it. Then they instructed him to just go with the king to Esther's dinner and be happy. Haman followed their counsel.

That evening, Xerxes had a raging case of insomnia and decided to read the chronicle of his reign. His eye caught the account of Mordecai's exposure of the conspiracy against his life, and he asked, "What honor and recognition has he received for this?" (Esther 6:3). Just then Haman arrived to request permission to hang Mordecai.

Still pondering a suitable honor for the latter, the king asked Haman,

"What should be done for the man the king delights to honor?" (v. 6). Thinking the king was referring to himself, he suggested that this deserving man should be given the king's royal robe and horse in preparation for a spectacular, one-man parade. What an ego!

The Unraveling Begins

Then came the kicker. The king ordered Haman, "Go at once ... get the robe and the horse and do just as you have suggested for Mordecai the Jew, who sits at the king's gate" (v. 10). A very disturbed Haman reluctantly followed Xerxes' orders.

Afterward, a grieving Haman rushed home to tell his wife and advisers what had transpired. They abruptly changed their tune, telling him to forget about taking out Mordecai, or *he* (Haman) would "come to ruin!" (v. 13). At that moment the king's eunuchs arrived to take him to Esther's shindig.

At the banquet, the king again asked Esther to state her request, promising that it would be granted. She responded by asking him to spare her people. Xerxes asked, "Where is the man who has dared to do such a thing? (Esther 7:5). Mustering all her nerve, Esther declared, "The adversary and enemy is this vile Haman" (v. 6).

Realizing he had been had, Haman began to beg for his life. Xerxes thought he was attempting to seduce Esther and blurted out, "Will he even molest the queen while she is with me in the house?" (v. 8). Then someone tapped the king on the shoulder and informed him of the gallows that had been erected for Mordecai. The king commanded, "Hang him on it!" (7:9). Immediately the deed was done.

Notice what occurred in the aftermath. Haman's estate was given to Esther, who in turn presented it to her cousin to oversee. Also, after Esther clarified her relationship with Mordecai, the king granted him carte blanche permission to enter his presence at will. Xerxes presented Mordecai with the very signet ring he had reclaimed from his would-be assassin!

Remembering her people, Esther successfully entreated the king to reverse the edict to annihilate them. Better yet, Xerxes had Mordecai do it with his full approval. Result? "For the Jews it was a time of happiness and joy, gladness and honor" (Esther 8:16).

Significance in Three Dimensions

According to my sociologist friend, Kent Olney, the Book of Esther could legitimately be the Book of Mordecai. He is an active player in nine of the ten chapters, and his name appears 20 percent more often than Esther's. Furthermore, while her significance is considerable, it occurred on a single level—that of success. Mordecai achieved significance on *three* levels.

Focusing on survival, he quietly and dutifully raised his orphaned cousin. Then, after she became queen and required a mild rebuke for fearing to approach the king on behalf of her people, he unhesitatingly offered one. That was crucially important for the Jews' continued survival.

Furthermore, when he learned of Haman's treacherous edict, he forthrightly displayed his grief by tearing his clothes, donning sackcloth, and loudly voicing his lament. And this occurred after he became aware of the gallows that were erected for him! Unquestionably, Mordecai achieved great significance at the survival level.

Then, for a brief period, Mordecai enjoyed a respite, giving him a season of stability. After Esther became queen, he stationed himself at the king's gate, where he monitored her, the nobles, and the king. Evidently, she slipped him enough to live on so that he no longer needed to be gainfully employed.

Prior to Haman, Mordecai's Jewish kinsmen seemed accepted and quite safe. His cousin had risen to the heights of royalty. Although nobody knew for a while that she was Jewish, folks were aware that he was her cousin and guardian. That provided him with a measure of respect. It was at this stage that he revealed the assassination plot, though it wasn't widely proclaimed or handsomely rewarded at the time.

But then, after Xerxes awakened to the great, lifesaving favor Mordecai had done for him, Mordecai reached the pinnacle of success. Everything Haman had connived to get was eventually given to Mordecai. Let's zero in on his final, well-deserved tribute contained in the last chapter of the Book of Esther.

King Xerxes imposed tribute throughout the empire, to its distant shores. And all his acts of power and might, together with a full account of the greatness of Mordecai to which the king had raised him, are they not written in the book of the annals of the kings of Media and Persia? Mordecai the Jew was second in rank to King Xerxes, preeminent among the Jews, and held in high esteem by his many fellow Jews, because he worked for the good of his people and spoke up for the welfare of all the Jews *(Esther 10:1-3)*.

Discussion Questions

1. Have you ever given something or done something for someone and had your good deed come back to you? Is this a law of life you count on?

2. Have you or somebody you've known achieved real significance while stuck on the survival level? How about at the success level? Please share.

3. Why do we delay seeking and attaining true significance until later in life? Do you know of someone younger who defies this tendency? Share.

4. Do you know any person like Donnie Moore, who gave up and became self-destructive after encountering a high-profile failure? How can we best guard against this?

5. Looking at his illustrious life, what single act of Mordecai do you judge to be the most significant? Why?

Action Items

1. Ask a random person if there is anything going on in his or her life you can pray about on his or her behalf.

2. Sit down and write a letter to the powers-that-be on behalf of someone or some segment of society that's being oppressed or ignored. One letter can mean more that you can possibly imagine.

Ten
No More One-upmanship
True Identity

Estimate the water volume of the ocean, the scorching temperature of the sun's surface, the distance to the farthest star. Try to wrap your brain around what our national debt might be in 50 years or when all disease will be expunged from earth or when universal peace might become a reality.

Arguably, these mind-draining questions pale in comparison to the difficulty of estimating the power of human influence. Call it what you will—clout, gravitas, weight, sway—our potential to impact others in the here-and-now is incalculable.

I recall my father saying, "Influence is that something you *think* you have until you go to use it." I think it's true, because I remember my friend trying to convince his teenage daughter to forego getting tattoos, and my neighbor trying to get his dog, Annie, to come back into the house.

Encarta World English Dictionary defines "influence" as (1) the power that somebody has to affect other people's thinking or actions by means of argument, example, or force of personality; (2) somebody or something able to affect the course of events or another's/others' thinking or action.

Even a casual observer notices the immediate power of influence in many normal, everyday incidents. For example, I've frequently heard it said that marital partners begin to look alike over the course of their marriage. I scoffed, but then I read the same conclusion in a social psychology textbook. What's the reason? Married couples continually see each others' facial expressions, causing their facial muscles to constrict similarly to those of their partner. The result is that—or so the theory states—their faces appear to have an ever-greater resemblance.

Another example of influence: In a classroom, someone coughs or blows his or her nose, and others immediately follow suit. Once again, we see evidence that the imitation trigger in brains is unconsciously squeezed. Monkey see, monkey do.

But often the attempt to influence others is deliberate. Have you ever been to a sporting event when a few start "the wave" by holding their arms in the air and rising to their feet? After a few false starts, invariably the wave begins to serpentine around the entire stadium, causing the originators to feel extremely influential.

Receiving More than Tacos

Here's another illustration of influence that might make you smile. I heard a story of a young lady who frequented a fast-food-drive-through, namely Taco Bell. On several occasions she gave the cashier an extra ten dollars and asked her to please use it to pay for the order of the people in the car behind her. If it was over ten dollars, then she asked the cashier to pay for the first car behind her with an order than totaled less than ten dollars. She asked the cashier to be sure to tell whoever had their order paid for to "pass it on."

I would have assumed that the folks behind her would seize the opportunity to pocket a little extra cash But here's how the story goes. After doing this a few times, the young lady drove up, and the cashier hollered to fellow employees, "She's here!" It seems the Taco Bell employees had started counting how many cars continued her chain of generosity. The record for one day was an incredible string of 23 drivers.

One girl dared to pass along a ten dollars worth of human kindness without disclosing her identity to recipients or seeking personal credit. And many followed her lead. Chalk it up to influence.

It's undeniable that influence enlightens us, inspires us, guides us, and nudges us to be kind. Unfortunately, influence also has the potential to turn dark and ugly—light years away from anything wholesome, endearing, noble, or commendable.

Spreading a Deadly Virus

The powerful influence of Adolph Hitler is well-documented. He charmed intelligent people with an outstanding cultural heritage to seethe with hatred and wreak unbelievable havoc. How he did it will always remain a great mystery.

It is sad to reflect on how much good might have been wrought by this ruthless, insane leader—*if* his influence, charisma, and intensity had been channeled in the right direction. It is tragic when people who are naturally gifted become obsessed with convincing others to do evil.

Consider Jim Jones, who used strychnine-laced Kool-Aid to choreograph 900 simultaneous suicides in Guyana; or Charles Manson, who cast his demonic spell on a group of girls then joined them in savagely murdering actress Sharon Tate and her friends. More recently, who can forget the terror that gripped our nation when John Allen Muhammed and John Lee Malvo—the juvenile he tutored in crime—committed countless random murders?

The old saw goes that it takes only one bad apple to spoil the whole bushel. It is a rule of our universe that each affects others, continuously and consistently, in positive or negative ways. In the same way, it is inescapable that the same is true of influence.

Sometimes what seems like a positive is merely an illusion, convincingly staged.

One Gigantic Smokescreen!

When it comes to imputing motives, I admit to having a definite weakness. I wouldn't consider purchasing the Brooklyn Bridge, but I can be bushwhacked by an honest-looking car dealer or a smooth-talking magazine salesman. I suspect that I'm not alone.

It's one thing to be fooled in face-to-face, up-close interaction with *individuals,* but have you ever been bamboozled by the slick pitches of huge corporations with big public relations budgets that stop at nothing to influence us to buy, support, excuse, vote, or whatever?

Influential? Absolutely. And most are legit. Consider the Geico Insurance Company's commercials that feature the little green gecko that speaks with an endearing Australian accent. Multitudes have been motivated to switch their insurance by that little character. I've heard that Geico's 1-800 number has received calls from persons saying they want to switch their coverage to "the company with the lizard."

But some corporations use the smoke-and-mirrors approach to influence us. Case in point: cigarette maker Philip Morris ran an advertising blitz solely intended to improve its image.

The tobacco giant had donated $2 million to domestic violence programs. Barred from advertising tobacco products on television, the company used its donation as a ploy to get back on the tube. Poignant stores of women who had been helped by the company's donation to violence shelters were portrayed. Philip Morris came off looking like the good guy.

It was discovered, though, that Philip Morris spent $108 million on advertising to tell the world about their $2 million gift. Do the math. That's 54 times the amount of the actual donation just so we would all know what a good corporate citizen this company is. Evidently, this is a standard practice for corporations under fire: use commercial "halo" speech to influence public opinion.

The campaign was a smokescreen, calculated to distract attention from the company's role in manufacturing, promoting, and selling a product that kills and sickens millions. Once these facts are known, Philip Morris's motives become very transparent.

Stash, Splash, Dash

The question these days isn't so much about whether we're a good or bad influence; the important thing is the *size* of our influence. That's why so many today aren't content to just make a mark—it must be a big mark. We yearn to become famous or, if necessary, infamous. We want to be a tsunami rather than a mere ripple.

The ultimate dream for many of us is to see our name on a marquee or on the cover of a bestseller. We want to make the evening news and grab our 15 minutes of fame. If successful, we want to squeeze every last drop of recognition for our success. We are not adverse to tooting our own horns or crowing about our importance as we seek opportunities to be visible.

Observe football fans who paint their faces with the team colors hoping to draw attention. If they think the television camera is pointed in their direction, they go nuts—leaping, screaming, pointing as if they've just won the lottery.

What explains that behavior? Why is it such a big deal to be noticed? Maybe it's because if people think we're a big deal we will have very satisfying rewards heaped upon us—both material and nonmaterial.

So we *stash* bucks, making certain others are made aware; make a *splash* with what we purchase to evoke envy or admiration; and *dash* around to make ourselves look important. Top movie stars are termed A-listers, and superstar athletes are referred to as franchise players. Every niche of life labels and lauds its best.

Most of us, though, will never hit the big time. I think that may be for the best, because most of us probably couldn't handle it. We might change for the worse—alienating those now close to us, or becoming so impressed without ourselves that we completely snuff-out our dependence on God.

SECTION 3

Not Giants, but Not Midgets

As normal, ordinary, maybe even deficient human beings, we still can make a significant impact on the world. Enough of us ripples, when combined with other like-minded ripples, can become a tsunami—if we work together.

Even as separate, uniquely-endowed individuals, our influence will count. Anyone who contributes to this world's good is always significant. His or her small acts and humble thoughts can be the seed from which promise grows.

Abe Lincoln alluded to this importance of a simple, meaningful act when he declared, "My goal in life is to plant a flower where a weed once grew." This former country lawyer as a youth observed slave trading in New Orleans. It so repulsed him that he vowed that if ever given the chance to uproot the weed of tyranny and plant the flower of freedom, he would. In the wise providence of God, he was eventually offered that opportunity.

I've been impressed by two others, neither headliners, who said something that clicked with young men and who later became world-renown evangelists. The first was Billy Sunday, who never forgot the kind words and glass of cold water given to him by a Sunday School teacher after he hit a homerun when he was a kid playing in a sandlot game.

Dwight L. Moody worked at one time as a shoe salesman in Chicago. While trying to fit a customer, the customer made the offhand remark, "The world has never seen what exploits God can accomplish through the person who is totally obedient to Him." Those words were indelibly etched on young Dwight's mind and heart. Right then and there, he decided that *he* would be that person.

Just as inspiring are ones I've known who didn't become great evangelists but were instrumental in persons finding the Lord. One was my college chum and world-class tennis player, Tom Wilkerson. He shared that a pastor he hardly knew, Virgil Rayburn, repeatedly came to the

Southgate High School gymnasium to watch him practice basketball. Tom, a star on the team, noticed that Rev. Rayburn hung around after practice to talk about nothing in particular—just regular stuff. A relationship was gradually formed that resulted in my friend accepting the Lord and attending our Christian college, where he became a star.

Harold was on the baseball team. As I recall the story, when Harold tagged a fellow out, the guy didn't take it too kindly. He threw a haymaker that landed squarely on Harold's schnoz. Harold, my uncle, hit the sod with blood spurting in all directions. But Harold was a Christian; he got up, brushed himself off, and walked away. He didn't believe in retaliation, even though he outsized his aggressor.

The opposing player who lost his cool never got over Harold's reaction. The next day he apologized and admitted that he wouldn't have brushed it off as Harold had done. Seizing a golden opportunity, Harold shared his faith, and the guy accepted Jesus into his heart. The one who refused to hit back ended up winning!

In all of these instances, influence wasn't pervasive because the influential were powerful, intelligent, or wealthy. By normal standards, they were fairly run-of-the-mill folks who, when it came to saying or doing the right things, had good hearts and great timing. Although none were top dogs, it is undeniable that the impact of their lives was extraordinary. Why? Because they allowed God to use them.

The world may judge our influence to be lighter than a feather. But that's because they use a wacky scale. The scales that are flawlessly accurate belong to our Heavenly Father. When He reigns supreme in our hearts, the weight of our influence is incalculable; what may appear as mere ounces in the eyes of the world can become tons.

How might our influence as His disciples be optimized to the limit? As we might expect, our focus is again on anonymous living and giving as we serve God and allow Him to direct that influence within us toward others.

Providence Always Trumps Promotion

We've seen that living for the applause of God alone maximizes many dimensions of joyful living: worship, eternal reward, and significance. To this list we now add influence.

If we use our influence to elicit personal acclaim—and we succeed—it can make others envious. But in a real sense, the self-promotion aspect is likely to make the apple of success taste bitter-sweet. Many follow this same course—elbowing and climbing over others to get ahead. It often lapses into the same old game of King of the Mountain—reeking with things such as driving ambition, self-centeredness, and end-justifies-the-means reasoning. In short, personal advancement to impress is deemed paramount, regardless of casualties and costs.

In sharp contrast, when believers purposely forego the adoration of the crowd, and that is picked up by others without the believers advertising their own good deeds, it can have a great, far-reaching impact. Specifically, it can cause a ripple effect that causes others to follow the same course.

When self-promotion is rejected, God is free to work unimpeded, and that can only result in good: inner joy, fulfillment, display of true Christian character, God-directed glory. Interestingly, the very thing show-offs most crave—great admiration, popularity, acclaim—is often attained by ones who crave and seek it least.

Schooled by My Student

Her name is Jessica Milazzo. I knew her as a brilliant student who always sported an infectious smile. She aspired to be a lawyer, and I've never known a student more qualified to enter the profession. Her future seemed exceedingly promising. From my vantage point, she was well on her way.

When Jessie was 12, misfortune struck. Her brother was diagnosed with autism, immediately immersing her family in the world of home-therapy, supplements, special diets, and speech therapy. As Jessie put it,

"Autism is often referred to as the 'silent epidemic,' yet its necessities rang out to us with assertive clarity."

As a result, Jessica's mother, fresh out of medical school, was unable to complete her residency. She ended up staying home and being a caretaker for ten years.

Finally, the plan was made to hire someone to provide assistance so that Jessie's mother could complete her residency and become a doctor. Then another setback occurred; a very painful divorce ensued. Jessie's mother had to shelve all of these plans once again in order to help provide financially for her family. This occurred just when Jessie was graduating from college.

Jessica declares that her mother never asked her to assume care for her brother so that she could finish her residency, but she prayed that God would put the idea in Jessie's heart. And that is what He did, prompting Jessica to put her own career on hold so that her mother could finish up.

Jessica went from graduation line to the daily grind of being a caregiver. Is she resentful? Is she angry that God allowed these heavy doses of tribulation? Not at all. Does she see her time of caretaking as a complete waste of time? You make the call after pondering her response:

> In truth, having an autistic brother has been a spiritual blessing. In place of pecuniary ambitions, I now hope to attend law school to help disabled children as a special education attorney. That would have been a hypocritical objective had I not first attended to the needs of my own brother.
>
> The months leading up to my decision were the most difficult. After asking everyone I knew for advice, an astounding majority counseled me to not put my career on hold. Now that I am here, though, I cannot imagine having made any other decision.

Although many aspects of Jessica's story are impressive, one fact impacts me the most. Never did Jessica broadcast her plight or her selfless decision. It was only after I accidentally heard talk of it and pleaded for her to supply me with the details that she reluctantly provide the entire account. It was very apparent that she intended her detour to be anonymous and secret.

Did her story have an uplifting, positive influence on my life? Absolutely. And I sincerely hope that it has a similar impact on yours.

Discussion Questions

1. What are the greatest non-human influences in your life? What persons—both close and distant—are or have been the most influential?

2. What valuable lessons can be taken from the Taco Bell story? Have you or someone you know ever originated or been involved in a similar "pass-it-on" incident?

3. Do you know of companies or persons who are guilty of doing what Philip Morris did—hyping a good deed in a way that is disproportionate to the actual value of the deed?

4. Why are we so quick to minimize the importance of the small, benevolent acts of ordinary people? Conversely, why are we so impressed by grandiose deeds? Can you recall when a small act meant much to you?

5. Have you known anyone who sidelined their plans, as Jessica did, to benefit others? Please share the results.

Action Items

1. Try doing something, on your own or with someone else, similar to what the young lady did at the Taco Bell. Monitor how it goes.

2. Offer to relieve someone who is providing ongoing care of another—such as a single mother or someone who takes care of a bedfast relative. Perhaps you can form a chain of helpers to cover more hours.

Eleven
Capturing True Humility
Deflation

Paul Bassett, renown church historian, is a respected friend and someone from whom I've learned much. In a phone conversation I shared with him that the theme of the book I was writing was anonymous living, and I invited his input. His first words were "Jon, your book is all about humility." Exactly. Paul had scored a bull's-eye.

Indeed, the person who prays, pays, and professes in secret, undergirded with a loving motive, is bound to possess humility. Pietism isn't about *seeming* or *appearing* saintly. Rather, it's feeling exceedingly privileged to talk to and inconspicuously serve the Lord, and that fills the person's heart with joy.

Folks often attested that my father, Leo, was a very humble fellow. He certainly had humble roots—an unspectacular life. Here is a brief bio on my dad.

Dad was the son of a southern Illinois coal miner, the oldest of eight children. He was forced to drop out of high school to work in the coal mine to help support his family. After God placed a call on his life, Dad completed his ministerial schooling, under hardship, at God's Bible School in Cincinnati. During his first pastorate, he and my mother took in laundry just to keep the wolf away from the door. He served as pastor in small churches in six different states during his ministerial career.

My father embraced humility, and one of the reasons may have been that according to the way success is measured in this world, he had very little to brag or swagger about. Sociologists would describe him as "status-deficient." That sounds better than "dirt poor." "Status-deficient" is the label sociologists use for someone who lacks all or most of the four currencies of status in our culture: power, privilege, prestige, and possessions. My father certainly lacked those things.

The people who impressed my dad the most were humble people. Some of them he knew personally or observed—folks ranging from high to low estate. Others whom he intently read about were historical figures like Lincoln, Ghandi, or Bible characters.

Dad never tired of reflecting on the deep meaning and wonderful dividends of authentic humility. He often piped up with things like "Son, always remember that real humility grows on the grave of pride." I soaked up his words like a sponge, for here was a man who walked his talk, frequently returning home minus articles of clothing he had given away to the destitute.

When I was in high school, he recommended that I read a certain book that, along with *The Christian's Secret of a Happy Life*, impacted my life more than any I've ever read outside of the Bible. The title of the inspirational Christian classic my dad recommended is *The Character of Jesus*, by Charles Edward Jefferson. And in keeping with my dad's character, his favorite chapter was the one that spoke of the humility of our gracious Lord.

You may be thinking that my childhood was heavy with "humility overload." But, on the other hand, since humility is the highest cardinal virtue, I think not. After all, "humble" is how our Lord described himself when proclaiming, "I am gentle and humble in heart" (Matthew 11:29).

It's fair to draw the conclusion that it would be impossible to receive an overabundance of enlightenment on humility.

From Fuzzy Comprehension to Clarity

It would be naive to suggest that humility is or ever has been universally sought and treasured. The unfortunate truth is that many fail even to grasp its true meaning. To paraphrase Charles Edward Jefferson, no other virtue is so misunderstood, erroneously defined, or persistently counterfeited and caricatured.

It has been that way for a very long time. If you or I could go back in time and be a cable television reporter and shove a microphone into the face of an ancient Athenian and ask, "What, in your view, is humility?" I believe the response would be startling and amusing.

Humility was considered to be on the same level as being a coward or being mean-spirited, and not only in ancient Greece. Throughout the entire pagan world there was no such virtue as humility. Furthermore, when persons were judged to manifest even slight traces of it, they were thought to be plagued with an incurably serious defect or blemish.

Our Lord personally took this ancient vice and transformed it into a lovely and lofty virtue. Nevertheless, even though He did this marvelous feat, being the slow learners that we are, many of us still don't get it. More specifically, we sometimes misinterpret humility to mean a low estimate of our qualities, so we feel short-changed and cheated; or we feel a sense of inferiority compared to others; or we think it's our lot in life to be imperfect and stuck in a web of desperation—and we succumb to softness, passivity, and a willingness to submit, accepting a milquetoast destiny.

Our Lord embodied the epitome of humility, so we would be wise to explore what he taught about it. His teaching is extremely clear, accurate, and reliable.

Humility 101

The Lord beamed the spotlight on three essential components of humility. And He vividly illustrated these by connecting them to situations He and His disciples experienced.

First, Jesus put a child in the midst of them and declared, "Whoever humbles himself like this child is the greatest in the kingdom of heaven (Matthew 18:4). And what is a young child's supreme characteristic? In a word, it's *freedom*—freedom from self-sufficiency and vanity. A child doesn't care about ambition or schmoozing with the elite.

The second component emerges from a gripping set of circumstances. Despite His admonitions, two disciples, pushed by their aggressive mother, displayed incredible selfish ambition, demanding to have positions of honor in His kingdom. Here is Jesus' response:

> You know that the rulers of the Gentiles lord it over them, and their high officials exercise authority over them. No so with you. Instead, whoever wants to become great among you must be your servant, and whoever wants to be first must be your slave—just as the Son of Man did not come to be served, but to serve, and to give his life as a ransom for many (*Matthew 20:25-28*).

With this straightforward instruction, Jesus struck another resounding note in humility's anthem. Indeed, humble persons stand ready to be helpful to those in need, often in ways that seem demeaning—like being stretched on the crossbar of a cruel cross.

The final component in humility comes from the 13th chapter of John's Gospel. The occasion was on the night of our Lord's betrayal as he shared His last supper with His disciples in the upper chamber. Without the slightest trace of pretense, He girded himself with a towel, grabbed a basin, and began washing the dust and grime from their feet.

He explained to them that as He had assumed the role of a slave to serve them, so they must sacrificially serve one another. His point was that humility implies laying aside our dignity, making ourselves of no reputation, and possessing a willingness to relinquish pride in order to experience the joy of loving service.

According to our Master, if we're to be authentically humble, we will

- possess a child's freedom from self-sufficiency and vanity;

- resist the Gentiles' obsession with being in control and strive instead to be useful;
- embrace the role of slave in order to serve.

Very few of us would boldly claim to measure up to our Lord's understanding of humility. At our best, we're works in progress, nurtured and led by the Holy Spirit, conscientiously seeking to manifest this crucial virtue in our everyday lives.

Unfortunately, many of us allow ourselves to be lured into swaggering, strutting pride. Our inflated self-image causes us to overlook our faults and accentuate our assets. If we continue on this course, it seems inevitable that we'll end up with egg on our faces. Even if we refuse to laugh at ourselves, others are certain to be amused—often mentioning our names around the water cooler.

When We Bust Our Britches

As a kid in southern Mississippi, I recall often hearing the term *comeuppance*—referring to a situation in which someone was too big for his or her britches and got cut down to size. I recall two stories when blowhards were force-fed a generous portion of humble pie.

A fellow was introduced at a meeting with profuse compliments. He believed them, causing his hat size to instantly expand—if you catch my drift. The next morning, while gazing at himself in the mirror, he yelled out to his wife, "Dear, just how many truly great men do you think there are in this world?" She crisply shot back, "One less than you think." Unmistakable comeuppance!

My late friend and superb editor Gene Van Note shared a story I've never forgotten. A newly commissioned captain received his first oceanic assignment, which made him feel downright heady. Finally his dream had come true—obviously because of his superior qualifications.

Shortly thereafter on a stormy night he spotted a light moving in toward his vessel. Feeling up to the challenge, he ordered the signal man to send a message. "Change your course 10 degrees to the south."

To his surprise, the reply came back: "Change *your* direction 10 degrees to the north."

What nerve! Determined to not give way to the other vessel, the captain sent this terse message: "Alter your direction 10 degrees to the south. I am the captain."

Promptly, the response flashed back: "Alter your direction. I am the lighthouse." The signal man snickered as his superior stormed off in a huff. Comeuppance!

It is ironic that the same ego that facilitates greatness can also prompt a downfall. "Pride goes before destruction, a haughty spirit before a fall" (Proverbs 16:18). At what point does ego become toxic? Precisely when it turns into arrogance or hubris—an inflated sense of self-importance. The following quotes concur.

"Those whom the gods destroy they first make proud" (Sophicles).

"After we place ourselves on a pedestal, any step we take is down" (James Dobson, paraphrased).

"When nature leaves a hole in a person's mind, she usually plasters it over with conceit" (Henry Wadsworth Longfellow).

"Pride is a lot like horse liniment—okay if not taken internally" (anonymous).

The Posture of His People

Christians can sometimes come across as distastefully arrogant. If we're self-righteous and give the impression that we're nearly immune from the infirmities and temptations that plague others, we ostracize folks who feel that we judge them to be unqualified to join our "holy club."

Such an attitude is blatantly unchristian. As I heard Rick Warren point out on "The Larry King Show," there's a reason why words "pride" and "sin" have the same middle letter—"I." Then he added, "It's not about us." Indeed, any value we possess is based solely on the generous grace given us by our Lord.

Scripture declares that any boasting we do must be in the Lord (see

1 Corinthians 1:31; 2 Corinthians 10:17-18; Psalm 44:8; 34:2-3), in the cross He bore (see Galatians 6:14), and in His Father's kindness, justice, and righteousness (see Jeremiah 9:23-24).

One and the Same

Paul Basset was right—the anonymous Christian life squares perfectly with biblical humility. If God's love motivates us to act, contribute, and pray in secret—as inconspicuous acts of worship directed to Him alone—we're not into feeding an insatiable, relentlessly driven ego. Otherwise, we would play to the crowd to evoke the acclaim and admiration of others.

By the same token, if we're into parading our piety, it's a sure indication that our ego is perpetually thirsty. Will it be satisfied? Maybe, but temporarily at best. People are fickle.

To chalk up big stats on heaven's scoreboard, we must do our good deeds away from the spotlight—for Him alone. If folks are unaware of our good deeds, we're not likely to become arrogant. And should they become aware of our good deeds through the providence of God—without our plotting or manipulation—our Heavenly Father is sure to receive the glory.

This spirit is very evident in a person whose refreshing and inspiring story was shared by my friend Ron Lush. As head of Global Initiatives, an organization that supports and encourages Christian leaders everywhere, Ron finds that his program is the recipient of many generous grants. While all are greatly appreciated, only a few of the donors specify that they wish no credit or acknowledgment.

But one person defied the odds. He directed a very large monetary gift to a Christian university, along with a very uncommon stipulation. He directed that it all go for "critical infrastructure"—plumbing, sewers, fire extinguishing systems, and so forth. These are low-profile but incredibly necessary materials that no one ever contributes toward! They're not flashy and conspicuous like buildings, fountains, and statues.

When asked if the organization could honor him by putting his name on something, the fellow responded with a playful grin, "Sure. I'd be very pleased if you'd go right ahead and inscribe my name on a fire hydrant far below ground level." The implication was, of course, that he wanted his recognition buried down deep where there would be no chance anybody would ever see it. What a vivid contrast with most who contribute, and a beautiful illustration of humility!

Here's a final admonition for all of us to seriously ponder, offered by Oswald Chambers in *My Utmost for His Highest:* "Beware of posing as a profound person; always remember: God came as a baby."

Discussion Questions

1. Like my dad, do your heroes tend to be humble persons? Or do you most admire self-promoting persons with big egos? Explain why this might be.

2. What are some really goofy notions about humility that you've come across? Might such ideas be a big reason why humble people aren't more greatly esteemed in our culture today? How about other possible reasons?

3. After reviewing our Lord's three lessons on humility that focused on a child, the Gentiles, and a slave, which one of these seems the most difficult to incorporate into your life? Why?

4. The Bible states that God despises six things, and the very first mentioned (Proverbs 6:17) is haughty eyes (or pride). Why do you suppose it is so detestable to Him, and conversely, why does He exalt humility so highly?

Action Items

1. Engage in loving and encouraging conversation with someone you strongly sense has a depleted self-concept. Cultivate his or her friendship. Should you feel led by God, seek to gently mentor the person to a sense of self-acceptance or even self-esteem.

2. This coming Christmas, encourage a child or grandchild—or yourself—to take a favorite gift you receive to someone you truly care about, possibly someone in need. Do this anonymously with only an unsigned note enclosed. Also, resist the temptation to tell anyone what you did or who you did it for. This can be done on other holidays—or on any day.

Twelve
Witnessing with Pizzazz
Effective Transmission

Recently I showed a video to my anthropology class that spotlighted Papua New Guinea—located in the eastern half of the world's second largest island—100 miles north of Australia's spectacular Barrier Reef.

Many of its inhabitants are primitive, especially in the rugged and inaccessible highlands. Shrouded beneath thick clouds and hidden in dense foliage, the tribal people are sheltered from the computerized, cell-phone-saturated world we know.

In 1964 missionary Wallace White began a five-day trek into the Papua New Guinea jungle. As he entered villages, the inhabitants scurried to hide, then slowly reappeared. White's countenance and words exuded Christ's love to such a degree that the people gradually began to trust him. From that trust, a great missionary enterprise has grown.

Do-gooders or Intruders?

Positive changes have occurred in the culture as a direct result of the missionary influence and example.

Tribal wars had been a longstanding tradition. Not only do missionaries care for casualties of these wars, but they have also introduced a game of bloodless mock battles to help folks peacefully act out their aggressions. Tribal deaths have plummeted.

The treatment of women was brutal. Women went off alone to give birth without the help of a doctor or midwife. Seventy-five percent of the children died before their fifth birthday. Also, fathers ignored newborns and even refused to have sex with their "unclean" mothers for two years.

Missionaries have come alongside the women of Papua New Guinea to make their lives more bearable. They have introduced birthing assistance. Although many women still go off into the bushes to have their babies, infant mortality has decreased to 25 percent. Also, men have been convinced to become caring team players in the lives of their wives and children.

Medical care was previously nonexistent. Today, Kudjip Nazarene Hospital treats an average of 6,000 patients each month, and patients pay only $8.00 regardless of the severity of their problem or length of their stay. Dr. James Radcliffe reflects the deep dedication of staff when declaring, "We treat the patient, for the patient's sake, in order to bring him or her joy."

In cooperation with the government, mission schools have greatly increased literacy. According to the country's prime minister, the teaching of morality—following conversions to Jesus—has sharply reduced crime.

This all adds up to significant assistance for a desperate land. Furthermore, there has been no push to rob Papua New Guineans of their distinctive culture. They are not forced to dress differently, and it is not demanded that they accept Jesus before receiving medical assistance; there is no arm twisting to get them to stop all tribal war.

As the video concluded, I was confident that the students would be convinced that missionaries can be a benevolent, non-paternalistic force. To verify this, I asked the students for their reactions.

Activating the Richter Scale

Hands shot up, but I was startled to hear that most expressed an abhorrence for what they had just seen.

"To change an indigenous culture in any way is to taint them with inferior ideals."

"It's pure self-righteousness, prejudice, and arrogance that motivates missionaries to use this bait to land conversions."

"By influencing these people to make changes, we really mess them up—giving them unrealistic expectations, encouraging dependency, and superimposing on them our polluted lifestyle and attitudes."

What galled these students, the majority of whom claimed to be Christians, the most? While mildly disapproving the advances we've mentioned, they vehemently objected to the fact that the members of the mission team shared their faith—even though it was done without the slightest trace of intimidation.

In short, inviting Papua New Guineans to accept Jesus into their hearts was considered appalling. The consensus of the students was that it implied that missionaries judged *their* belief system to be superior when in reality the one the islanders possessed had served them well for thousands of years.

So I asked "Are you declaring that Christians should refrain from sharing their faith?" Nobody answered, and that troubled me greatly. I asked if they were aware that God's Word repeatedly declares the absolute necessity of true believers sharing their faith. That, too, was met with blank looks and no responses. These students weren't about to allow reason to alter their emotional attachment to the to-each-his-own, postmodern predisposition.

Wincing at Witnessing

It was obvious that the gist of our contention focused squarely on the issue of witnessing—or the sharing of our faith with the intention of converting others. Phineas F. Bresee, founder of the Church of the Nazarene, defined it as "telling fellow beggars where to find the Bread of Life."

Despite what my students might think or were afraid to declare before their peers, witnessing must be the spontaneous, natural response of those who have been granted salvation. In an article "Breakfast with the Pope," which appeared in the December 1995 issue of *Christianity Today*,

Pope John Paul II pulled no punches: "No true Christian can keep his or her faith hidden as a personal matter. For such an encounter with the living God cries out to be shared—like the light that shines, like the yeast that leavens the whole mass of dough."

Our faith must be spilled out, disclosed, revealed, shared, passed on. Doing so allows us to be effective ambassadors of Christ, which results in souls being won and ourselves being fulfilled. As my friend Larry White puts it, "In the final essence, the Church only gathers in order to scatter." By scattering the Good News far and wide, we testify to a skeptical world that we treasure our faith and deeply care about the eternal welfare of others.

We could never expect an unbeliever to concur with this. But well-known atheist of yesteryear Robert Green Ingersoll acknowledged that all authentic Christians will witness often and intensely.

His belief was that Christians would do all within their power to rescue someone stranded in a burning building. It should follow then, he asserted, that if they really believed in the never-extinguished flames of an eternal hell, it's logical to assume that they would take drastic measures to keep persons from going there by boldly and persistently witnessing. Following that logic, Ingersoll concluded that because most Christians don't witness, they must not believe what they say they believe.

There are flaws in his argument, but unfairly or not, it stands that he indicted the entire Christian community because of its deficiency of witness. According to recent statistics, only one unbeliever is converted annually for every 400 Christians on the average each year. That means that only two percent of us are winning one person per year. If we attempted to run a business with that success rate, we would go broke.

We, like Peter and Andrew, are called upon to be "fishers of men." (See Matthew 4:19.) Does the extent of our fishing consist of casting bait at targets within the four walls of our churches? Do we use all sorts of excuses for not actually getting our lines wet where lost fish reside? We should hunger to share our faith. This is indeed an important litmus test of the vibrancy and authenticity of our love for Jesus.

There is a real danger in refusing to witness. "Whoever acknowledges me before men, I will also acknowledge him before my Father in heaven. But whoever disowns me before men, I will disown him before my Father in heaven" (Matthew 10:32).

In his article titled "Ponder This," which appeared in *New Man* in the March/April 2003 edition, world-renown author Rick Warren declared that there are only two things we can do on earth that we are unable to do in heaven. One of them is to *sin,* and the other is to *witness.* He says that God surely didn't leave us here to sin, so we're created to pass on the good news of salvation to nonbelievers.

Once we're convinced we must witness and commit to do so, we must determine the best way to go about it.

Choosing the Best Strategy

Of course, many Christians witness, and many do so in very creative ways, as did first-century believers who shared their faith by drawing the universally recognized fish, a Christian symbol, in the sand. If repressive authorities came close as they were witnessing, it could be quickly and easily scratched out.

I heard of a well-intentioned barber in recent times who sought to share his faith with a captive audience—one of his customers. His timing and word choice were less than ideal, though. Just after sharpening his razor, while holding it close to the guy's throat in preparation for a shave, he gave the fellow a serious look and asked, "Sir, are you prepared to die?"

Other creative attempts have backfired as well. Some years back, the movie *The Gospel Blimp* portrayed sincere Christians sending up dirigibles with Scripture verses painted on the sides. Unfortunately, they blocked TV reception, and citizens became irate at the perpetrators. As a result, predictably, the public was totally non-receptive to the message.

On a trip to Jerusalem our guide shared a story. She stated that some well-meaning Christians were in a heap of trouble, having been hauled before the city magistrates. There is a group of orthodox male Jews who walk single file and pray at the same time each morning on a sidewalk along the city wall. To insure that their concentration isn't broken by seeing an attractive female, these fellows discipline themselves to stare down at the sidewalk while walking.

The band of Christians noticed this and, desiring to get through to them with the gospel, came up with a plan. One morning, an hour before the Jews customarily walked, they scotch-taped messages along the entire length of the sidewalk. They figured that the men, looking down, would have no choice but to read the godly messages. The men read the messages all right, but their reactions weren't nearly as positive or redemptive as the Christians had anticipated.

There are, though, creative ways to witness that are inoffensive. Those of us who watch NFL games on television often see a witness banner held up behind the goalpost when a field goal or extra point is attempted. It usually contains words such as "John 3:16" or "YOU MUST BE BORN AGAIN." Since fans hold up signs for most anything—some truly inappropriate—to communicate to the vast TV audience, this simple Christian statement seems very subtle and inoffensive— perhaps even effective.

A well-known group, Jews for Jesus, employs all sorts of creative methods to witness to their Hebrew brethren. These talented folks present plays, sidewalk carnivals and puppet shows, and they even finance dinners at fancy venues for the purpose of kindly and discretely proclaiming that the Messiah has truly come. The results of their efforts have been nothing short of amazing.

The Talk with the Walk

There are two important components of witnessing. First, we must *proclaim* proactively. First Peter 3:15 tells us "Always be prepared to give an answer to everyone who asks you to give the reason for the hope that you have." The psalmist declares: "Let the redeemed of the Lord say so" (Psalm 107:2).

Being a silent witness is not sufficient. The simple and unmistakable fact is that most of the billions in our world who do not know Christ will not come and ask us to explain our beliefs. We must take the initiative to go to them.

We must intentionally enter the space of others with the message that our Lord "came to seek and to save the lost" (Luke 19:10). Likewise, as Jude candidly declares, it behooves His disciples to "save others by snatching them out of the fire" (Jude 23).

To do this guarantees that we will often be condemned, as Paul and the apostles were. On a recent program of "Larry King Live," I heard a nonbeliever denounce the president of the Southern Baptist Convention for being a bigot because he embraced an only-through-Christ-are-we-saved position.

Speaking up has always been a challenge. I receive a weekly "Persecution Alert" e-mail that lists fellow Christians around the world who are enduring harassment. Most of the incidents involve my brothers and sisters who are merely sharing their faith in the countries where it is against the law and is labeled "an attempt to proselytize." Punishments meted-out (by legal and other disagreeing citizens) are often incredibly harsh—involving physical attacks, burnings of churches, and long imprisonments.

I spoke with a 60-year-old saintly man who had been incarcerated along the Mongolian border for 21 years. He testified to instigating revivals in the hearts of fellow prisoners and even guards. At the time we spoke, he was under house arrest in Beijing. Was his witness stifled? No way. Each week he wrote sermons that were read from pulpits of three large churches in China's capital.

In addition to proclamation, we must selflessly live out our faith by involving ourselves in *good deeds*. It's the other side of the Christian coin. Paraphrasing a well-known quote by Francis of Assisi: "Witness at all times. If necessary, use words."

I am grateful that evangelicals have discovered the AIDS challenge, and pray that scores will devote themselves to lifelong service with such marginalized groups as the mentally ill, homeless, neglected, and also the poor. As Moses and Jesus both reminded us, we will always have the poor with us, implying that our responsibility for those who are impoverished never ends.

When the world sees us involved in noble acts of service and improving justice, it can only make our words more effective. Best of all, we are accepting the towel of servanthood that our Lord entreated us to accept on the night of His betrayal. To identify with His service and suffering, even in a small way, is guaranteed to overwhelm our hearts with joy.

But how does authentic, anonymous living, motivated by love for our Heavenly Father, relate to effective witnessing?

Undercover Agents of Good News

In churches I attended during my childhood, we regularly had what we termed "testimony meetings." At these times, individual congregants stood and briefly shared whatever they wished. Many spoke of trials they were facing. Others shared inspirational thoughts that had come to them. Still others praised the Lord for specific answers to prayer. Usually it was a blessed time of sharing.

However, I distinctly recall a few who used the opportunity to heap praise upon themselves. Using this venue as a stage, they cleverly conveyed the impression that everything was glowing in their lives and that this was due to either (a) their own skill or intelligence or (b) their being a favorite son or daughter of God. For them, this was an opportunity to brag, swagger, and gloat. To be honest, they came across as self-righteous blowhards—resulting in the rest of us feeling depreciated in worth.

That's the effect of self-promotion. Others are not elevated in spirit; rather, they're made to feel "less than," inferior, second-class. Does the boaster receive acclaim? Often. But such acclaim is his or her reward—paid in full—in this world. And his or her witness is severely depreciated.

Besides, such a person sets a bad example. I recall that occasionally in our testimony meetings, after hearing the exploits of a self-promoter, another would take the bait and subsequently do his or her public bragging. It turned in to a competitive top-this-if-you-can session of vanity in which giving glory to God seemed a postscript, if even that.

What a contrast from the anonymous servant who quietly goes about being faithful, whose every act of love and kindness is intended solely as an act of worship and praise to his or her Maker! Such a person shies away from the limelight, plays down acclaim that might surface, and is internally at peace. His or her security lies in the relationship with God, not in the positive, fickle reactions of others.

We all know what typically occurs when the anonymous liver and giver is outed and others are made aware of the person's extreme sacrifice or generosity. It is a fantastic witness. It wasn't contrived or calculated on the basis of expected payback. It was done simply because the person felt it was the right thing to do.

In a world of folks continuously looking for press, paparazzi, power, privilege, and prestige, such an individual stands out like a teenager at an AARP convention. Result? The impact is far-reaching.

It Wouldn't Stay Secret

Often those who serve anonymously are not fully discovered or appreciated until after they die. When folks converge to pay them tribute and recount touching stories of their selfless deeds, the impact can be powerful.

I was a college kid who, along with my peers, felt myself invincible. We were young and healthy, anticipated great futures, and not weighed down with many adult responsibilities. Our greatest concerns seemed to be getting a date for the next social event and getting the money to pay for it. World events? I don't recall even reading the newspaper.

Then, without warning, four of my buddies climbed in a car for an evening of fun. There was a terrible freeway accident, and Tom Maxwell was killed.

The entire student body and faculty were devastated. Tom, a tall, good-looking guy, was greatly esteemed by all. He was fun to be with, was a fine student, and had lots of friends. He was solidly Christian. We were all very sad. As stories were remembered, the distinct profile of a Christian who served anonymously surfaced. Here was a guy who went about quietly and consistently doing good and reflecting the fruit of the Spirit—but never in a showy manner; strictly low key.

A fellow from our city, unaffiliated with the college, stepped forward to share a story that deeply impressed my youthful mind. Just a few days before the fateful accident, Tom had initiated a redemptive conversation with the guy, presented the gospel to him, and invited the man to accept Jesus as Savior. They shared a brief prayer together, and the man departed as a new creation in Christ.

This same fellow heard of the accident and was grieved by Tom's untimely passing. He connected with our community and paid loving tribute to the person who helped usher him into the Kingdom.

We hadn't known about this. Tom hadn't rushed back to brag in a testimony meeting; he hadn't even mentioned it to best friends. It was between him and God alone.

When this anonymous act was revealed, many of us were blessed and were provided with a memorable story to help guide us in the days ahead.

Discussion Questions

1. Share any indications you may have picked up that, in an attempt to be nonjudgmental, our culture is increasingly hesitant to tolerate the belief that Jesus is the only gateway to salvation. If so, what might be our best approach in witnessing?

2. Do you feel that witnessing is optional for Christians? Does the Bible seem to agree with your conclusion? If you and the Bible disagree, how is this best resolved?

3. Concerning witnessing strategies, what specific approaches have you encountered that appear counterproductive? What creative strategies have seemed especially effective?

SECTION 3

4. What are reasons so few verbally witness today? Why are people in society increasingly less responsive to verbal witnessing?

5. Why do believers appear to polarize on articulating the plan of salvation vs. the doing-noble-deeds mode of witnessing, gravitating toward one or the other rather than doing both?

6. Why must, and how might, this one-sidedness be corrected?

Action Items

1. Print onto cards that are small enough to fit in a wallet, or write out on paper, the following:

[On side one write]

To Become a Christian, I Must Understand—

1. Like everyone else, I have sinned.
   For all have sinned and come short of the glory of God (Romans 3:23).
2. Left unchecked, sin will eventually doom me.
   For the wages of sin is death (Romans 6:23)
3. Jesus was crucified so my sins can be forgiven, and I can have eternal life.
   For God so loved the world that He gave His only begotten Son, that whosoever believeth in Him shall not perish but have eternal life (John 3:16).
4. My part? Confess my sin and believe that Jesus cleanses my heart, as He promised to do.
   If we confess our sin, He is faithful and just to forgive us our sin, and to cleanse us from all unrighteousness (1 John 1:9).

[On side two write:]

My Prayer to Become a Christian

Jesus, thank you for dying on the Cross so that I can be forgiven of my sin and become your child. At this moment I ask you to cleanse my heart of all sin and make me pure. Thank you for hearing and answering my prayer. I now accept that I belong to you, not just in this life but for all eternity. In the days ahead, please help me to follow your guidance and to influence others to accept you as their Lord, as I have done today. In Jesus' name I pray. Amen.

Distribute these anonymously as opportunity allows and as the Holy Spirit guides you.

2. With paper and pen, write out what you would like for people to say about you after you pass away—especially as it relates to Matthew 6. Consider showing this to a trusted and candid friend and ask him or her how close you seem to be to this ideal.

Thirteen
Leaving the Best Legacy
Footprints

Florence Nightingale, English nurse and founder of modern nursing, sensed God's call to service at the tender age of 16. She began taking food and medicine to poor farmers and intently focusing on nursing in spite of her family's ardent objections to her pursuing what they considered a menial vocation.

When she was 30 years old, she wrote in her diary, "God asked me if I would do good for Him alone without concern for reputation." She responded by surrendering herself to His will, journeying to Europe for nurse training, then serving as director of a London hospital for women.

During the Crimean War (1854-56), Florence organized a unit of 38 field nurses. This nursing care revolutionized army medical care, greatly reducing mortality rates and bringing about strict hygiene standards and procedures.

After the war, in spite of a hero's welcome awaiting her, she was somehow able to slip back unnoticed and went directly to a convent to spend a full day in solitude and prayer, offering gratitude and seeking guidance. She needed to refuel but did so quietly, alone and in secret.

Shortly thereafter, she again faced the public to begin an aggressive, successful campaign to urge health reform legislation. This compassion-driven pioneer went on to found the first school for professional nurse training, wrote books on nursing and hospital administration, worked to establish commissions on health and sanitation, and helped found the army medical college and first military hospital.

Her own health eventually failed from overwork, and she spent her later life as an invalid, though still fighting for improved medical care and conditions. Florence Nightingale died at the age of 90. At her request, her tombstone read simply "F. N. 1820-1910." That was to be expected; being simple and inconspicuous was her signature style.

Florence Nightingale avoided the spotlight, but this humble servant left a very significant footprint. Since her passing, the Florence Nightingale Pledge has been and is recited by millions as they receive their nursing licenses.

Florence left an enormous legacy for good, but not by being blustery and ostentatious. She had neither time nor inclination to engage in egregious self-promotion. Her quiet, steady life more closely resembled a silent, incredibly powerful, rising tide—the kind that lifts ships of heavy tonnage—rather than a frothy but far-less-powerful riptide. She had "gravitas," or, as some might put it, her life cut a huge swath.

Legacy: Influence in the Next Dimension

Legacy extends beyond mortal life. It's that lasting impression we leave upon our departure from planet earth. Put another way, it's that something about us that's remembered—for good or ill.

Popular speaker and author Anthony Campolo, in a sermon titled "If I Had to Live It Over Again," recounted a study that zeroed in on 50 persons over the age of 95. These old-timers were asked what they would do differently if they could live their lives over again. It was expected that the replies would be all over the map. Not so. These three dominant themes, stated in a variety of ways, surfaced:

1. I would reflect more.
2. I would risk more.
3. I would do more things that will live on after I'm dead.

The third change on the list relates directly to leaving a legacy. These seniors wish they had intentionally focused more time, attention, and energy on how they would be remembered. They wanted some part of them to live on and that their lives would count for good.

We would be very wise to intentionally focus on the legacy we're building. The earlier we start to think about what kind of legacy we'll leave, the better. With this in mind, I regularly assign a project to my university students requiring them to write their own hypothetical epitaphs—one they might wish to have read about them at their funerals.

As a follow up, I ask them to write a personal life plan that's congruent with that epitaph. The idea is to first construct the hoped-for ideal, then come up with a specific pathway that will lead to that reality. The results are often amusing—especially for those expressing hopes of being remembered as party animal or the shrewdest rich businessperson on the planet!

In terms of legacy aspirations, the older people focused more on *regrets*, while the students set their sights on *hopes*. Still, there's remarkable overlap between the two groups on one key issue. Both groups adamantly concurred that our lives should leave a track record of *significance*, a record that surpasses success and attains authentic excellence. I wrote more on this subject in my book *Christian Excellence: Alternative to Success*.

The senior adult group and the student group both proclaimed that our lives should consist of more than breathing, eating, and procreating during our appointed "fourscore and ten." In short, we must be fully alive! Many persons fail to grasp this crucial truth.

As former German chancellor Konrad Adenauer observed, "We all live under the same sky, but we don't all have the same horizon."

Others buy into this ideal for a while and then seem to become diverted or exhausted. As someone said, "Many of us cash it in long before we tuck it in." We mistakenly see our lives as a sprints rather than marathons and thus peak prematurely. We make our fortunes, rise to the heights in our professions, win perfect spouses. Then, after concluding that we've made our dreams come true, we slouch into becoming zombies—still breathing but for all practical purposes deceased—or at least comatose. I'm reminded of an epitaph Chuck Swindoll ran across that described one such person: "DIED AT 30; LIVED TO 65."

Understandably, settling for a life of mere existence—a prolonged vegetative state—seems to make our approaching death a much harder pill to swallow. As George Washington Carver said, "No individual has any right to come into the world and go out of it without leaving behind him distinct and legitimate reasons for having passed through it."

If that holds true for humanity in general, it's doubly so for those of us who claim to serve the one who left behind the greatest legacy ever—our Lord and Savior.

Two Kinds of Legacy

Legacy is usually seen as having two key dimensions, or put another way, as casting two kinds of shadows. The first is spread widely and directly relates to how folks, most of whom are strangers to us, perceive our image or persona. This especially comes into play if we've attained a measure of fame or notoriety, as propagated by the media or history books.

If I asked who "the king" refers to, many of us would answer "Elvis Presley!" That's because we've repeatedly heard him called that by the media. His image shadow doggedly persists. But the same is true for well-known gangsters like Mickey Cohen and John Dillinger.

The point is simple: once someone's persona is indelibly etched in the minds of many, it usually endures. That's precisely the kind of legacy the masses crave and covet. For such persons, the thought of dying, being given a celebrity funeral, and being remembered for a larger-than-life image is to hit life's jackpot.

The second kind of legacy relates to the "small shadows" our lives casts upon persons we've been intimately involved with. In sociology, we refer to the latter as "significant others"—persons who are certain to grieve intensely when we're gone. Our influence on their lives crystallizes into a permanent footprint—they'll carry a part of us with them until they die.

Not long ago I listened as my friend Pat, a widow, described her late husband's continued impact on her life. Much of what she said seemed surreal. Harvey's picture remained beside her bed. His clothes still hung undisturbed in the closet. Even the things he had left around the house were right where he left them. She couldn't bear the thought of diminishing his presence. I must admit to being a tad creeped out when she spoke of pausing to ask Harvey for his help in locating misplaced car keys.

Unless we've felt the ongoing impact of the life of someone close to us who has died, we find it hard to grasp this feeling. It is more visceral than cognitive. Ask the multi-million-dollar sports star I heard interviewed whose own broad shadow legacy is assured. In the interview he passionately expressed how he is aware of his late father's presence, now more intensely felt than ever. He said that each day he pauses to reflect on his incredible dad and the kind of life he lived.

I've observed persons in the throes of making an important decision. While someone waits to hear what the person has decided, he or she says something like "I need to think about what my mother would have advised me to do." Truly, the legacy shadow casts a deep and abiding footprint—and imprint—on such persons.

Sadly, the legacy of a significant other can also be unpleasant. We may, for example, relive the nightmare that a departed abuser or neglector caused. Hard as we try, we're unable to expunge from our memories a lingering and crippling negativity. In cases like this, sometimes even the best counseling or psychotherapy doesn't provide much relief.

In a television interview a few days after his father's passing, I heard

American Idol singer Clay Aiken respond to this question: "Clay, why didn't you attend your father's funeral? While it was going on, you were just blocks away giving a concert." With steel-cold eyes, the young entertainer, who had often alluded to his father's abusive antics, said, "That person who died was nothing more than my sperm donor." It was apparent that the deep hurt and scars perpetrated by Clay's dad continued to be vividly recalled and intensely felt.

So far, we have discussed two kinds of legacy. Both are powerful but very different in important ways. Perhaps, this summary chart may provide additional clarity:

	#1 BIG SHADOW	#2 SMALL SHADOWS
breadth/scope *	wide	narrow
relationships	secondary (generalized others)	primary (significant others)
intensity	less impact/ superficial	greater impact
longevity	longer time span	less (after 2nd generation)
accuracy	less (constructed image	more (direct contact)

For those of us who call ourselves Christians, however, a crucial third dimension of legacy exists.

Legacy's Third Dimension— In a League of Its Own

The first two dimensions resemble each other in a key way. Their focus is squarely on persons our lives have impacted. This final dimension of legacy focuses exclusively on our Heavenly Father.

In the final essence, everything pales in comparison to what He thinks of us. To paraphrase my plainspoken neighbor, Hall of Fame manager Sparky Anderson, "There's only one score that should really matter to us, and that's what the Scorekeeper in the Sky writes beside our name."

Some play to the crowd. Others seem intent, as noble as it may seem, on leaving a positive and uplifting legacy for family members and friends.

But both of these legacies are, at best, only temporary. By contrast, when our deepest intention is to please God alone, our legacy investment yields eternal dividends. And our lives are truly joyful.

In so doing, we're offering Him the purest kind of worship. It's direct—rather than being filtered through the reactions or approval of others. He alone is who we're seeking to please. And why not? It's our blessed Lord who has earned our praise by sending Jesus to die for our sins. When we by faith accept Him as our Savior, it's He who permanently inscribes our names in the Book of Life. This guarantees our by-invitation-only entrance into heaven.

We see another great dividend of living a life directed toward fashioning a godly legacy for Him. When we do so, we present His Spirit with a much higher grade of materials to work with. Minus the mixed motives inherent in constructing a legacy for ourselves or others, we're presenting Him with a virtual blank check to use as He sees fit.

What's the best way to formulate and present our legacy to Him, then? Once again, we can focus attention on those timely, crucial verses in Matthew 6—the ones in which Jesus repeatedly declares that it's best to give in secret, to be quiet and inconspicuous, to disregard the opinions of others, and to avoid the solicitation of their praise.

Intentional, Purposeful Anonymity

Our culture trumpets the importance of the individual—his or her pleasure, accomplishments, and rights. In so doing, we diminish the primacy of the family, group, or society. Plainly put, it's a raging case of me-centeredness or narcissism. Here are the signature profile traits of a typical narcissist:

Lives for the present. He or she thinks, *All I have is right now, for tomorrow may never come. Therefore, I'll grab all the gusto I can.* Since confidence in the future is absent, the narcissistic parent gives little attention to his or her children—they represent the next generation.

Has an insatiable craving for consumption. The idea that one can make oneself over—a new appearance, a new personality—excites the narcissist. And without inner resources, the narcissist absorbs the characteristics of what he or she buys.

Must have an admiring audience. The narcissist dreams of being a perpetual performer drawing constant applause. If the dream is realized, he or she feeds on the glamour and excitement that celebrities receive.

Charms people in order to manipulate them. Playing the game is the narcissist's natural response to internal urges. He or she is typically witty and vivacious, but once people recognize that skill and the narcissist is rewarded, he or she becomes restless and bored, often treating former admirers with contempt.

Lacks emotional depth. The narcissist's feelings tend to ebb and flow. Quick flare-ups of emotion are followed by sudden quiet. He or she is unable to adequately experience feelings of sadness, mournful longing, and depression. The latter are replaced by anger, revengeful wishes, and resentment.

Feels entitled to special favors without earning them. Rewards are demanded, and he or she feels surprised or angry when the demands aren't met. He or she is preoccupied with fantasy and feels that unlimited success, power, brilliance, beauty, or ideal love are just around the corner (Barbara Rowes, "Gratification Now Is the Slogan of the 70s, Laments a Historian" [an interview with Christopher Lasch], *People*, July 9, 1979).

This prevailing principle of honoring individual pleasures, accomplishments, and rights is evident within our academic community where those caught plagiarizing are soundly chastised. A sizeable number of natural scientists, for instance, have initiated litigation to ensure that a legitimate individual is credited and/or rewarded for an initial discovery or creation.

But a significant number of ancient/medieval authors apparently felt no such compunction to showcase their individual exploits or merits. They did not boast or strut whatsoever. In fact, many resorted to publishing works in the real or fictitious names of *other* people. Some affirmed persons they respected by elaborating on or enlarging upon what the persons had said or written in an attempt to duck the spotlight, grab it, and turn it to beam on another.

Anonymity was embraced as a value and strategy for very noble, selfless reasons—exuding humility by invoking another's authority—waking up Christendom to its destructive course and passing on teachings and practices believed to be helpful. All were served up to God alone as pure and loving gifts of worship.

The world loudly proclaims—Leave a resounding legacy behind by ambitiously promoting yourself and your achievements while on earth. The persons referred to above saw it differently. For them, primacy was placed on burying, or not disclosing, any semblance of personal identity.

You may very well be wondering, *Isn't the term "anonymous legacy" an oxymoron? How can we possibly be remembered without full revelation of who we are, what we produce, and what we stand for? Isn't a personal attachment essential for a legacy to even exist?*

Go figure. We've just finished lauding folks who contributed much and followed our Lord closely. But in this author's thinking, their quintessential quality was their intentional willingness to remain anonymous. Why? Because, by *not* soliciting self-praise, they brought glory to the God they so faithfully served.

May we strive to fashion a worthy legacy that will honor and glorify our Heavenly Father. And in making this our cardinal goal, may we come to realize the supreme value of incorporating love-guided anonymity.

If you happen to be wondering, the answer is "yes." A legacy replete with anonymous acts of kindness, generosity, and service does live on—eternally. It yields an abundance of joy in both earth and heaven.

Before moving on, please pause long enough to thoughtfully ponder these cryptic and convicting words of J. M. Barrie from Barrie's book *The Little Minister* and repeated in John Maxwell's book *From Success to Significance:*

> *The life of every man*
> *is a diary in which*
> *he means to*
> *write one story*
> *and writes another;*
> *and his humblest hour*
> *is when he compares*
> *the volume as it is*
> *with what he hoped*
> *to make it.*
> —J. M. Barrie

Discussion Questions

1. What single fact about Florence Nightingale impresses you the most? Why? How do you process the words of her diary prayer?

2. If you could live your life over again, what would you attempt to do differently? Be specific. Compare your responses with the three predominant ones offered by the senior citizens in the study Anthony Campolo cited.

3. Have you been tempted to quit too early in life, or have you known people who did so? What are some thoughts that can help us keep going toward great goals and at full speed?

4. Review the three kinds of legacy presented. Which one do you most aspire for and why? Toward which one are you presently investing the most time, effort, and possessions?

5. What is your take on the authors who hid their identities? Did they go too far? In addition to the one in heaven, how can a person who lives and gives anonymously even hope to leave a legacy on earth?

Action Items
1. Start your own unique legacy in your community.
   - Begin helping an aged neighbor with yard upkeep.
   - Repeatedly give some money to the cashier of the local ice cream parlor to pay for a few cones for the next kids who come in.
   - On your walk around the neighborhood, leave notes of gratitude. You might express a thank-you to your neighbors for such things as maintaining a beautiful garden, refurbishing their house to the benefit of the entire community, or other similar things.

2. Telephone someone who is special to your life and tell him or her—not to request a favor, cultivate a compliment, or offer unsolicited advice—that his or her life means something special to you. Be prepared to make follow-up calls periodically if led by God's Spirit.

Conclusion

For most of Albert Einstein's life, he displayed just two pictures. Both were those of well-respected scientists—Sir Isaac Newton and John Clerk Maxwell. Einstein proclaimed that these giants of science were the ones who inspired him most. Then, to the surprise of everyone around, he abruptly removed these two pictures and replaced them with large photographs of Albert Schweitzer and Mahatma Gandhi. When asked why, he said he needed new role models—not of success but of humble service.

Who are your role models, your idols? Who do you consider to be the primary inspiration and embodiment of your highest ideals?

We need to ask ourselves if we truly embrace the greatest role model, the foot-washing, burden-bearing Servant—the one that God's Word repeatedly admonishes us to become like.

To accept Him as our role model implies something very important, that we're committed to becoming like Him, selflessly serving others anonymously. In His Sermon on the Mount, judged by multitudes to be the greatest discourse ever spoken on earth, Christ commanded us to do likewise.

The reason for this is clear: when we indulge in love-motivated, anonymous living and giving, we offer the optimum amount of glory to our Heavenly Father.

I believe that most of us grasp this vital truth. There's nothing really ambiguous or complicated about it. And that's the problem: our comprehension of our Lord's instruction is precisely what makes us responsible for incorporating it in our daily lives. To know is to be held accountable.

I recall something Mark Twain is reputed to have said: "It's not what I *don't* understand about the Bible that worries me—it's what I *do* understand!"

While continuing to parade our piety, some of us try to squirm out of feeling guilty by convincing ourselves that we're just exhibiting a Christian example for others to behold. To put that in today's language: that does not compute biblically.

In our heart of hearts we know well that at some point in our lives we must exchange our pride for humility. Our conniving to showboat must be replaced with servanthood. Our strutting performance must give way to quiet, inconspicuous demeanor. And rationalizations for not taking this course must be put aside. It's time to face up to the wisdom, rightness, and necessity of embracing our Lord's brand of rewarding anonymity.

A Chinese proverb declares, "If we don't change the direction we're going, we're likely to end up where we're headed." When we recognize that we're headed down the wrong road, the only right option is to make a U-turn. Another proverb, this one Turkish, simply advises, "No matter how far you have gone on a wrong road, turn back."

The incredible dividends of living such a life are incalculable. We will, without a doubt, have more personal joy while on this earth and will spread it widely. And we can anticipate in heaven an incredibly joyful celebration in the presence of the one we have faithfully served.

> *When you were born,*
> *you cried and the world rejoiced.*
> *Live your life in such a manner*
> *that when you die,*
> *the world cries and you rejoice!*
> —Author unknown